THE COMING

A. BEN BACON

THE COMING

A. BEN BACON

Copyright © 2024 by A Ben Bacon

ARPress
45 Dan Road Suite 5
Canton MA 02021
Hotline: 1(888) 821-0229
Fax: 1(508) 545-7580

Ordering Information:
Quantity sales. Special discounts are available on quantity purchases by corporations, associations, and others. For details, contact the publisher at the address above.

Printed in the United States of America.

ISBN-13:   Softcover   979-8-89389-111-9
                eBook   979-8-89389-110-2

Library of Congress Control Number: 2024909024

TABIE OF CONTENTS

"As I sat there quietly holding the twins that could save the world one day, a news story on TV caught my attention."

The Coming
by A. Ben Bacon

Joseph Everlasting is a dedicated and caring military veteran who is thirty years old. One day, he encounters his old friend from high school, Mary, in a difficult situation. Mary, who is pregnant with twins and facing a threat from dangerous individuals, confides in Joseph. She believes that her children are God's children and saviors and asks for Joseph's protection. Mary proposes that they marry and that her children take on his last name. After praying for guidance, Joseph firmly commits to marrying Mary and vows to protect her and her children at all costs. He is determined to take whatever steps are necessary to ensure the safety of his new family. In his compelling literary masterpiece, Bacon masterfully delves into the profound intricacies of selflessness, as depicted by individuals who unconditionally prioritize the well-being of others. These remarkable individuals exhibit an unwavering commitment toward placing the needs of others above their own, particularly when their actions are guided by an unshakeable faith in God. They showcase extraordinary courage and unyielding dedication in the face of adversity, faithfully carrying out what they believe to be God's plan. Through vivid and revealing dialogue, the characters' distinct and multifaceted personalities are intricately brought to life. For instance, Joseph emerges as a multidimensional character, embodying qualities of courage, compassion, and an unyielding sense of purpose as he tirelessly extends assistance to others without seeking anything in return. Within the captivating narrative, the book's numerous unexpected twists and turns ensure that readers are continuously engrossed, eagerly anticipating each new revelation.

- Recommended by the US Review

The Coming is dedicated to God and his saving me. In 2017, I was diagnosed with a traumatic brain injury after multiple falls. My neurologist told me that the odds were that I would probably never function normally.

But for some reason, after about four months of heavy sedation with 3600 mg/day of gabapentin, something or someone in my head said, "Stop!" And taking that as a possible interjection from God; after one month, I was off the medication and feeling more like myself.

My neurologist almost had an epileptic shock when I told him I had stopped the medication. In fact, when I actually told him, he quietly left the exam room, screamed his head off, came back into the room, and said, "Well, since you are still alive, we will go forward.

Within six months, I went from rolling out of bed and crawling to the living room to running mountain trails, snow skiing, and writing.

Looking back on my work on my first book, Cam's Dragon, published in 2019, I now saw what looked like elementary school writing, but with a lot of help from my publisher at that time, I was able to produce a readable product and heal my brain at the same time.

Now, The Coming and The Coming – Hunted, to be published in 2024, are yours to read and enjoy, and I thank God that I can.

CHAPTER ONE

It had been a long day, starting well before dawn, and it did not start well. A carpenter job, which would be well-paying and help me get through the winter, had been rescheduled for the spring due to financing, or so they said. So, at that point, I decided to go out hunting. And from the looks of the sky, I could expect some snow by late afternoon, especially where I was headed to hunt.

It was a good day for hunting. I got to my favorite spot just at sunrise, and by three in the afternoon, I had a spike elk and a forked buck mule deer. So, what started as a bummer of a day turned out to be okay. I would have enough food on the meat side of eating to get through the winter. And if I stocked up on staples, I should ride it out without real problems.

By the time I got back to the highway, it was after dark. As I headed west, snow came down hard, and the winds were almost at blizzard speeds.

Then, up ahead, on the side of the road, was an Indian woman, a Navajo looking at how she was dressed, hitchhiking. As a rule, I did not usually pick up hitchhikers, but the traffic was almost nonexistent, and I knew if I didn't pick her up, she would probably freeze to death. So I slowed down, and she climbed in and said, "Thanks; I wasn't sure if I was going to make it out there as hard as it is snowing now."

With the roads getting so bad, I knew I could not take her where she needed to go. I could tell that she knew the roads were terrible as well, and she asked, "Do you live very far away?"

I said, "About seven miles off the road to the right, about a quarter of a mile ahead. My house is substantial and should get through this storm easily. I have a spare room with a twin bed you can sleep in tonight. The room is warm, and I can wake you up whenever you like. And then I can drop you off in the morning on the way into Cortez to look for work."

She said, "Okay," and then was quiet. Tears flowed down her face as I turned right and headed back into the forest. She hung her head and said, "I am not that kind of a woman."

I said, "Look at me; I am not that kind of man, so just relax. I will have you home in the morning, and it will be like we never met, okay?"

She smiled at me and said, "I'm very sorry."

"There is no need to be sorry, no need at all. I can feel the pride it took to tell me that, and I respect an honest person, be it a man or a woman.

We drove silently for about fifteen minutes, and then I said, "Here we are, the door is unlocked, and if you can cook, there is food in the refrigerator."

Then I also said, "And if you can cook, please cook something up; I am starving! I forgot my lunch this morning, and right now, 'I could eat a horse and the rider that rode in on it.' I have a small elk and deer in the back that I must skin and hang. And if you like liver and onions, brown up some bacon and fry it with the onions. I'll follow you in with the livers. You can cook one and freeze the other for another meal. There are a few potatoes in the refrigerator if you want to throw them in, too." Her smile grew as she exited the truck and headed into the house. I followed her in with the livers and then went to the barn to hang and skin the deer and elk.

It took me a while to skin and clean them, and then I had to ensure they were covered and that the barn was shut and locked so the coyotes or wolves couldn't get in and rip the meat from the rafters, taking off with what should easily feed me through the winter.

I walked into the house, and to my utter surprise, the living room was straightened so that I almost didn't recognize it as my place. Keeping a clean house was not a high priority for me as a single man.

But what caught my attention was coming from the stove. The smell was heavenly, to say the least, and not just because I was starving! What that woman did with what she had to work with was excellent. She looked me up and down and said, "If you are going to sit at this table, you have to be clean, and you, by the way, what is your name?"

"Joe, short for Joseph. I chuckled; my mom Marion, 'May God keep her and my dad Peter, as promised,' was a Christian lady."

"Well, Joe, my name is Red. Now get cleaned up and make it quick. Dinner is hot and ready!"

Over the meal, which was delicious, I learned that Red had just lost her husband of thirty years and was on her way to Cortez to look for work in town when I picked her up. Then, as she again hung her head, she said, "Prospects are not great, though, being an Indian of my age." Then I sat there for a while and thought, as usual, before speaking, which has kept me out of trouble more than once. I looked around the house and said, "Red, and I know this is going to sound crazy, and this isn't charity, but if you want, you can live here through the winter, and come spring, we will see what God brings if that is okay with you?"

Red, thinking to herself. *That sounds crazy to me as well, Joe. But God works in mysterious ways, and this is one of them. And as strange as it sounds, he seems a man of his word, and damn it, I think I can trust him;* she smiled softly and said, "Yes. Joe, I knew you were a good man, and I am again sorry I had to say . . ."

"Don't mention it again. So, it is a deal; you cook and clean, and I will try to keep us stocked up for winter. Deal?" With tears rolling down her cheeks, Red said, "It is a deal, Joe!" That is how Red and I became friends. A friend like I never knew I would ever need.

Like I said, the deer and the young elk, with a few staples from the store, could get me through the winter. But now, with two mouths to feed, it would be tight, really tight! As predicted, the winter was cold and bitter.

As luck would have it, we were snowed in most of December, January, and February. We would have been in a world of hurt if it hadn't been for a young bull elk. He happened to kill himself when he slipped and broke his neck, trying to jump my fence to get at the alfalfa I spread out for Duke and Daisy. But as my mother always said, "If you are in need, God will provide."

Looking back, I think that was the best elk I have ever had! And speaking of being snowed in, it was December, and Christmas was just around the corner. Store-bought Christmas presents were out of the question. To solve that problem, Red and I devised a plan to make each other a little something in the way of a present to stick under the tree to be opened on Christmas Eve.

The plan included us braving the storm, finding the 'perfect' Christmas tree, and then decorating it with homemade ornaments, like in the old days. Red liked our Christmas Eve plan, but I could tell something was wrong in her mind. So I asked her, "What is troubling you about our Christmas Eve plans?"

She turned away and was quiet for a while before she started speaking softly. She said, "Do you believe? Do you believe that Jesus came to this earth, died upon the cross for our sins, and then rose from the grave with the promise to come back one day to judge us?"

Now, it was my turn to be quiet. I thought to myself, *Do I believe? God is always with me, especially when I am out in the forest and awed by his work. I believe in him in every new birth, whether man, plant, or animal. I am one to go to church on special occasions such as Christmas, Easter, and Christenings of new babies. But am I a true died-in-the-wool believer? To be truthful, I do not know.*

After deliberation with myself, I told her just that. Then she said, "It is what I expected of a man like you. And it isn't a condemnation of you at all. It is just you. Even as you said before, that very religious parents raised you. You have your doubts, questions, whatever, and I do not, and will not, ever hold them against you. You will decide when the time comes."

Then she continued, "I was raised in a Catholic school on the reservation and accepted Christ at an early age. So, in essence, I have always been a believer. That said, I have one additional request for our Christmas Eve celebration.

I want to read the story of Jesus's birth for myself and you. You were raised as you were; you probably know it by heart, but it is essential to me. Is that okay with you?" And I said, "Yes, by all means! It would mean much to my parents and me if you would." She said, "Thank you."

As Christmas Eve got closer, Red was as giddy as a child! There was a package under the tree with my name on it, but nothing for her yet, and I know she noticed. Because I saw her looking when she thought I couldn't see her. I was still working on it, and it was delicate work, even for a craftsman like me. That I had been stuck on what to make for her for a long time didn't help. And when it finally came to me, I wasn't sure I could finish it in time.

I came up with a hand-carved rose made from some deep red cedar. It would have one open blossom, two leaves, and even a thorn to remind her of her personality. I worked on it for several days, a couple of evenings, and early Christmas Eve morning; she had her present under the tree. And just from her slight attitude change, I knew she noticed the package.

The evening fell, and the blizzard rocked even my well-built home. We ate a great dinner and even had a bottle of wine I had stashed away for a special occasion like this. Then we sat in front of the fireplace, and Red read the story of Jesus's birth with such emotion that I couldn't help but be in awe. Then came the present time, and she insisted I open her gift first. I tried to object but to no avail. My hands were shaking as I opened the present from Red. Inside was a small box containing a deerskin pouch with "Joe" embroidered in beads. And she excitedly said, "Open it."

I pulled open the drawstrings and pulled out a piece of turquoise with gold veins running through it. It was hung on a thin leather thong to be tied around one's neck.

"Red," I said, "Beautiful beyond belief, and I truly mean it." Then I said to Red, "Your turn," as I handed her the gift I had so painstakingly made. She took a deep breath, slowly opened the box, unwrapped the paper, and stared at the rose. I said, "If you don't like it, I can make you something else?"

She gently picked it up and said in a very childlike voice, "Joe, this is the most special gift anyone has ever, and I mean truly ever given me. Thank you from the bottom of my heart. I will cherish this rose forever!"

And then she blushed a deep red as she said, "This is how I got my name." She slowly stood up and pulled up her skirt, and high on her right thigh was the birthmark of what could easily have been a red rose.

The skirt fell quickly like it never happened, and she said, "Time for a toast. To Joe and Red, and the most special Christmas Eve ever." We both drank our wine, poured another, and drank that one as well, with each of us, not knowing how special a Christmas Eve could be.

I should tell you about my ranch! It is just over forty acres, with mostly cliffs on each side of a valley, so the farming potential is near zero. But in Colorado, any piece of land over forty acres qualifies as a farm, and the land taxes are much lower. You have to make a specific dollar amount of improvements each year to maintain that lower tax status, which isn't that hard to do. Last summer, I put a bridge over a nice little creek that flows through the middle of the ranch, which was my yearly improvement.

While we were snowed in, I, being a carpenter, decided to build and put up a sign naming the ranch. So, even though I worked on it in December and January, it wasn't finished until spring so it would qualify as my improvement for next year. Two large oak trees were planted long ago on each driveway side. I figured they were planted by the property's original owners well over one hundred years ago because the trees were about fifty feet tall and should, with no problem, support my ranch sign.

I started with a twenty-five-foot by ten-inch wide and six-inch thick piece of oak. It was a ceiling rafter left over from a job several years ago. So, I got out my carving tools and went to work. It took me a while, but it came out nice if I say so myself. It read "Everlasting Home" since my last name was "Everlasting."

And let me tell you, I caught all kinds of hell in high school with the last name of Everlasting. That one I blame on my father, Peter Everlasting! Now that I think about it, he got teased even more than I ever did! Anyway, the sign had a carved horse on each end and would have a cross on top made out of some beautiful red cedar I had found up near Mesa Verde. It had grown in the natural shape of a cross, and with a bit of shaping and sanding, it looked damn good! That is, if you can say a cross looks damn good!

Because of the cold, I finished the cross in the cabin, and it glowed like it had a life of its own. After a day or so of drying near the fireplace, I headed out to the workshop to see how it would look on the sign and how I would attach it. As I was working, Red came into the barn workshop and asked, "Why Everlasting?" And before I could answer, it dawned on her, and she said, "You are Joseph Everlasting." I said, "Yes, and if I tell you this tidbit, you have to swear never to tell another living soul, promise?"

Red smiled and then paused. She looked at the sign, smiled, and said, "It is Joseph Peter Everlasting, isn't it!"

"Get out of my workshop now and never come back!" I yelled, smiling as she ran out of the workshop, laughing her head off.

There was still downtime, even working on the sign, feeding the horses, and keeping the walkway to the barn clear of snow. So, being an outstanding chess player, I taught Red the game. It was straightforward to beat her at first. But she had a sharp and intuitive mind, and soon, the games were usually entirely dual of wits. I still won most of the time, but believe me, I had to work harder and harder every game.

But as nature always has her way, spring came along and pushed winter away for another year. And that is when the real work of a ranch begins. And to Red's credit, she was no slacker! She was out cleaning out ditches for the alfalfa, helping to mend fences, not to mention bringing up the idea of a garden. The wild crocus plants were pushing their beautiful purple heads up through the leftover snow while the grass and the alfalfa were starting to come up nicely, especially alongside the creek. And the horses appreciated that fresh grass and the alfalfa, especially after a long winter of dried alfalfa from last year's harvest.

And lo and behold, the job canceled last fall came to fruition and would start in about three weeks. It was for a furniture store in Cortez that would handle rustic and elegant furniture. The store's interior must reflect that in all aspects, from floor to ceiling. And I was just the man for the job. The funny thing is that neither of us mentioned our agreement for Red to look for a job in Cortez come spring. I guess God has his plan for all of us, after all.

Red picked out her garden plot, and we fenced it in to keep the deer, rabbits, and all other creatures out. And it just so happened that I had a friend digging some footings for a new barn down in the river bottom and had rich soil he needed to get rid of. Red was so overjoyed that she cried all the way home with the first load of soil. That was until we came to the ranch sign. This was the first time she had been driven under it, and she burst into laughter, saying it should say, "The Everlasting Peter Ranch!"

I stopped the truck and said, "You can walk from here," she was still laughing as she headed for the house. We hauled five more truckloads, and she still chuckled, albeit quietly, every time we drove under the sign. I still feel bad for my dad!

I started work that following Monday and came home to Red out in the garden with a shovel and a hoe, working her tail off to get the garden ready to plant. Two weeks later, on payday, I surprised her with a rototiller. You would have thought she had died and gone to heaven. Tears of joy rolled down her face as she hugged me tight and said, "I was the best friend she had ever had," then I hugged her back, crying as well. To this day, that rototiller was the best investment I have ever made!

Red took to that garden like a mother hen to her chicks. She had plenty of fertilizer from the horses, cows, and calf I bought. So, along with nature's fertilizer and the rich river bottom soil, the garden was ready for planting in quick order. So for the next few nights, we discussed, or should I say I discussed, and she decided what she would grow.

On my next payday, we headed for the nursery. It took us, or should I again say her, about two long hours to decide on every variety of her chosen vegetables they had to offer, and I mean, every variety they had to offer before we left. And since it was still early spring, she bought mainly seeds and a few hardy plants that could withstand an occasional light frost. I swear she looked at every seed package in the house. At this point, it was beginning to dawn on me that this garden was Red's project and that the only part I was going to play in her project was the part of the brute force laborer." After coming to that conclusion, even though laboring was still my part, I figured I had better find my project.

Without mentioning anything to Red, my project quickly took shape in my mind. I decided to design and build myself, with the help of a local building contractor, a new bedroom on the house. Red could have mine, not that she hadn't made that small spare room her haven, but we needed a place for the occasional guest to spend the night. We didn't have many guests, but the few we had got the couch if they spent the night.

So, I started planning. There were four essential items I wanted in my room. First, I wanted a majestic view of the La Plata Mountains to the east. That meant a picture window, or two windows split by a corner fireplace, and item number two, a fireplace. So, I decided on the split picture windows option, divided by a unique corner fireplace.

The third thing was my bathroom. It would have a custom bath for soaking, a large shower with a glass shower door, and dual sinks, just in case I ever meet the right woman. Yeah, right.

The fourth item was a nice-sized closet lined in cedar. The northern end of the closet would be mine, with the right side of it designed to hold my hidden gun safe behind a wall covered in cedar, with a hidden release to access the safe.

I had all the framing wood I needed from various jobs, so that wasn't a problem. I even had the total makings of a nice bathroom, compliments of a wealthy oil guy who thought he knew what he wanted in a bathroom and ordered it. That was before measuring to see if it would fit the plans, which it didn't. The vendor wouldn't take it back because it was a particular order, so he said take it, and I did. I didn't know what to do with it, but I could sell it if nothing else. And I like it and think it will look great in my new bedroom.

So I have about half of what I need for the room. So, I will need a plumber, electrician, roofer, and a concrete/fireplace guy to do the rest of my project.

I have the money from my parent's estate after they died in a car accident. A drunk driver hit them head-on between Durango and

Farmington. At least if they had to die, they died instantly. Believe me; with God as my witness, I would rather not have a single cent, except what I worked for, and have them alive instead.

My ranch is all paid for, and this bedroom will be as well, and I will still have money left for emergencies in that account from my parent's estate. My other account is my work account, a checking account I use regularly for all my purchases. It holds all the money that I work hard for.

But my dad always told me to have some money in reserve because you never knew when and why you would need it. So, out of every paycheck, no matter how large or how small, 25 percent went into my private savings account first. And that was before any other purchase, no matter how important some other thing was, or at least seemed to be. And I have always stuck by that rule with only one exception. As they say, whoever 'they' are, there is an exception to every rule!

My job at the furniture store took most of my time, but I did get a much-needed benefit. I got a pair of husky/wolf puppies. One snow white and the other black as coal. The husky eyes gave that part of the parentage away, while the long legs and lean bodies decried the wolf side of the family. They would make great dogs if trained well. Red was ecstatic! And as luck would have it, they took to her like a tick to a hound. She named them Snow and Coal. They grew fast and were her shadows from then on.

I waited a few more weeks to ensure the chance of a hard freeze was very remote, especially when pouring concrete. But before that, to start a project for a room addition, you need to go to the county planning commission to get approval of your plans. I got my authorization relatively quickly since I had been in the trades for several years and knew the ins and outs of building.

So, with the approved plans in hand, I called a friend of mine, Hector, who owns a company that handles concrete, plumbing, roofing, and electrical work. They even have a genius in a unique fireplace design. You tell him what you want, and he can build it. It was like one-stop construction shopping!

We went to lunch at a local dive with great food, which only locals go to because it isn't on the beaten path through town. Hector went through the plans with an experienced eye and had only a few essential changes. He told me that since it was early in the building season, he had workers just waiting to return after the long, hard winter. And he said he would give me the builder's rate, which is about a 25 percent discount overall. A handshake was all the agreement needed to start, and I had workers at my place the following week.

Red was shocked as all the equipment rolled into the yard and said, "Joe, what is going on?" I looked at her and then at her garden and said, "You have a project; I also needed one! I am building myself a new bedroom. You are moving into mine, and yours will be remodeled into a guest room."

Red just shook her head and returned to her garden, mumbling, "Crazy white man?"

Red's garden produced like nobody's business. From dawn to dusk, she canned or frozen the earlier vegetables. As a bonus for the crews, she sent home fresh food to their families every day they were there. I think they were unfortunate when the job came to an end.

The bedroom took shape quickly, and I worked my tail off on the weekends to keep up with his crew. In the northeast corner of the room, the footings, plumbing, and concrete backing for my unique fireplace were built to be designed and built in the future.

I framed the room in one long weekend. Then the roof went on, and the exterior walls were finished, so the rest was up to me. At this point, it was nice to be working at my own pace. But even then, it came together quickly, which was good because Red was turning my old room into her domain. All the finer points in my new room would take much longer, but it had been a blast in the long run, with a great result. The fireplace would come later once I decided what I wanted it to look like. I told the mason, Manuel, my general idea, and he had the backing in place, just waiting for the finishing stonework on the front and up the chimney.

And talk about another pleasing result on the ranch! My stallion Duke had been a very busy boy during the winter, and I had my hands complete with two new foals, which were downright beautiful! The foals will be sold later in spring.

My ranch was growing by leaps and bounds, and as I sat on the porch one evening with Red, I said, "You know, Red, I don't think life can get much better than this."

Red looked at me and said, "You need a woman!" Then she got up and went to bed.

I thought to myself, *Joe, she is right! But as busy as you are every single day, the question is, what are you going to do about it?* Shaking my head, I got up and went to bed as well. Again, Mom's favorite saying popped into my head. She always said, "If you need it, God will provide."

Summer was warm but pleasant overall, without any real problems cropping up. And as the aspens turned golden and the air in the morning became crisp, my next real job, if you called it a job, was the guided hunting trip I did for the same group of guys every year. It was a great time, resulting in an outstanding group of friends being together for several years.

The guys came each year as much to hunt as to get away from life and enjoy friends of those many years. But this year, I had a twist to surprise them with. We had a camp cook, which freed up my time for other things. Red was coming with us.

They were a little hesitant at first. But the first night, she cooked a stew with a concoction of all her fresh-out-of-the-garden veggies and a combination of spices she only knew how to use. And magically, she was now one of the guys! Her stories at the fire kept everyone hanging on her every word. The trip, as always, resulted in plenty of meat for our freezer, as some of the hunters were there for a trophy deer or elk, both of which we got this year.

The new, now young colts even got into the mix in that they hauled light loads to and from camp and were especially a hit with two new additions to the group. Dick and Jane were their names. An older boy and girl accompanied their dad for the first time this year. The jokes about the two of them, Dick and Jane, kept the company in high spirits to camp.

My favorite was when Charles yelled back to the two of them, "Dick, Jane, I think you left Spot back at the house! Don't you think you guys should rush back and get him?" Everyone burst out laughing, well, everyone that is except Dick and Jane.

But the next day, they both got their revenge. Jane was the only one with a bull elk tag, and just so happened, she got a remarkable shot off, with a 30-30, mind you, and dropped a massive bull with a single shot that caught him right behind the ear. He never felt a thing. It took four of us to get it back to camp. And Dick dropped an eight-point buck not three hundred feet from camp. And as luck would have it, those two were the only ones with a kill under their belts that first day. The rest did well the next few days, so the trip was a marvelous success. Especially the second night's dinner. After Red cooked the elk back strap so well, she asked "if everyone was full."

When everyone shook their heads yes, Red said, "Too bad, I had a special treat for tonight, but if you all are too full . . ." and then came a resounding "no." Red pulled out two blueberry pies, with blueberries, out of her garden. In addition, and to this day, I don't know how she pulled it off, but she served it with ice cream as well! It was as if everyone hadn't eaten in days! They devoured the pie and ice cream with rave reviews for the cook!

The tips this year were so good for three main reasons. First, the addition of Red and her cooking, especially the pies and ice cream, the colts, and Red's dogs. Not to forget the trophy elk and mule deer that Jane and Dick, respectively, bagged.

I went to split the tips with Red, but she refused to take any, saying just being part of that adventure was enough for her. But that was before I reminded her of a very 'womanly' bed down at the furniture store, which she kept returning to admire when she was there. And then, she relented and took her share. (The bed in her bedroom looks great.) This trip will be one of the best memories in the group.

CHAPTER TWO

It had been a long last day of work, but it had been worth it. I started work at 5:00 AM and finished up early. Every room looked great and reflected the furniture already placed in each one. The owner was pleased because it was done before Thanksgiving, and Christmas was approaching. He was counting on good sales throughout the rest of the year and into the New Year.

I had dropped my truck off to have my studded snow tires put on because Red said, "I have a strong feeling you're going to need them tonight on the way home." And boy, was she right. As agreed, I finished up at work and got my final paycheck, with a nice bonus for finishing early. I walked to the bank and deposited 25 percent of it into my requisite savings account. I had secretly put Red on all my accounts, just in case!

I walked over and picked up my truck and noticed that the air temperature had already dropped significantly. Even though it was still raining in Cortez, I lived about 1,500 feet higher in elevation, which made a difference in the storms.

Red had given me a list of staples, including a turkey for Thanksgiving and stuff like dish soap, wine for the holiday meal, and rubbing alcohol for disinfectant. The rubbing alcohol puzzled me, but I had given up on second-guessing Red a long time ago.

So, I stopped at the liquor store and bought some pretty good wine and a small bottle of whiskey to celebrate the completion of a job well done. Then, I went to the grocery store, and if the storm turned out to be a strong one, I filled up gas and propane tanks, just in case. By this time, it was dark, and the rain was switching over to freezing rain. I have got to give it to Red, I thought; she was right; I would need my studded tires if nothing else than to get up the hill at the Mesa Verde entrance and all the other ones before my turn-off.

When I got to the first hill, the freezing rain had turned into very wet and heavy snow. Snow on black ice is the worst condition for driving on a mountainous road. Luckily, traffic was light, and I had no trouble until I topped the last rise near my turn-off and headed down the east side. That is when all hell broke loose!

Not for me, but for a car on the other side of the valley. From my point of view, I could see the car spinning out of control. I knew if I accelerated, even with the studded snow tires, I would be in the same predicament as the car.

Just ahead of the car was a sharp hairpin turn without a guardrail due to a semi-trailer truck plunging over the side in a fiery crash last week. And it looked like history was going to repeat itself. But as I watched, the car hit what was left of the damaged guardrail head-on and stopped!

Flames were starting to emerge from under the vehicle as it hung precariously, with the front of it dangling over the cliff. At this point, I threw caution to the wind and raced to help the poor souls in the car. That is, if I could get there before the vehicle became fully engulfed in flame and exploded. Time seemed to stand still as I raced up the hill, slammed on my brakes, and spun 180 degrees. My truck luckily came to rest against the next guardrail. As I ran to the car, one person was out, a pregnant woman who looked familiar, and another who seemed familiar, slumped over the steering wheel, not moving.

I grabbed the moving woman by the arms and immediately recognized her—Mareilene Johnson, a twin to the other woman in the car, Dareilene Johnson. I had known them both all through high school. I had no idea what they were doing here, but I knew I had to get Dareilene out before the car exploded.

As I moved to enter the vehicle, Mareilene grabbed me, pulled me back, and screamed, "She and the baby are already dead, and she needed help to push the car off the cliff and let it explode with them in it."

I screamed, "What in the 'Fuck' are you talking about? You can't do that!"

"Yes, I can." And she said, "Damn it, Joe, they're already dead, and the cars on my tail will be here in the next twenty minutes, or sooner, and I must be gone.

They don't know about Dareilene being my twin. It will take them off my trail. Now, you either help me, and me and my baby will have a chance to live with you, Joseph, or we all will die! God damn it, make up your mind and make it up fast. Dareilene and her baby are dead; trust me, I know these things, and I promise I will explain all of this to you because on this earth right now, God sent you here to save me and, more importantly, my baby. And according to 'him,' you are the only person he and I can trust!"

I looked into her eyes and knew she was telling the truth. She took her purse with her ID and anything else tied to it, threw it in the car, grabbed Dareilene's purse and suitcase, and headed for my truck. With the ice and snow and the car half over the cliff, it slid off the edge with a simple push just as it exploded. Mareilene threw her sister's suitcase in the truck and said, "Drive like the Devil is on your heels because he is!"

My turn was only a mile from the wreck, and with the snow falling at this rate, my tracks and theirs were almost already covered. Mareilene was bleeding badly, so while driving, I grabbed the first aid kit out of the glove box and said, "Grab some gauze and press it hard against your forehead. Check your baby's heartbeat! Is it regular?"

She said, "Fast, but yes, it is fine."

I said, "Put the seat back now because you will be going into shock much sooner than I can get you home. Do it now." She was already showing signs of shock, and I said, "Get your feet up on the dash to keep the blood to the baby and your core."

She was already starting to move slowly but doing what I said. "Good girl, Mary!" I spoke. Mary was what I called her in high school, just like everybody else. I turned the radio on loud to keep her awake and drove like she said, "Like the devil was on my tail," and I could tell she truly believed that!

At this point, I had no reason not to believe her. I looked at the crucifix dangling from my rearview mirror and said directly to God, "If You wanted me to help her, you damn well better help me get her home, and I added a big AMEN since I figured after what I had just done, it couldn't hurt.

Meanwhile, at the crash site, three black Suburbans pulled into the open space at the top of the curve, drawn by the flames coming up from the valley floor. And last but not least, out of the third Suburban stepped a man dressed all in black. He had a sharp, pointed beard, which he slowly stroked as he walked over to the driver of the first Suburban and said, "You and your group will stay behind. When the police arrive, and they will, you will tell them you saw the car ahead of you spinning out of control, hit the guardrail, and plummet off the cliff.

That and nothing more. Understand?"

The man bowed in reverence and said, "Yes, Master."

Then the man said, "We will continue into the next town; I think it is called Cortez. After the police are done with you, meet up with us there, as you will 'know' where we are as soon as you come into town. We have work tomorrow to ensure the 'Who' we are searching for is dead! You have your instructions. And you know the consequence if you, or anyone with you, makes a mistake that leads them to me. Again, do I make myself 'perfectly' clear?" As the snow and ice melt below his feet, as he walked back to the last Suburban."

The man again bows and says, "Yes, Master."

The police arrive about a half hour later and survey the scene, take statements from the men, and then, after again looking at the wreckage in the valley below, ascertain that no one, not even God himself, could have lived through that. With that, the patrolman sent the men on their way to Cortez. He then called for an ambulance along with a wrecker to remove the burned-out car from the valley floor as well as the victim inside of it. The patrolman, whose night was already long and still had at least four hours to go, got into his car and headed toward Durango, where he was headed in the first place.

As I reached the house, Mary had just passed out, and there was nothing I could do about it. I knew that for Mary, it was now the most dangerous time for victims of shock, especially pregnant shock victims. I jumped out of my truck and yelled at the top of my lungs, "Red, get the hell out here; I need your help, NOW!"

Red came sprinting out of the house, already in her nightgown and robe, but as she saw the passed-out woman in my arms, she knew time was not in her favor. She looked at the woman, and she was very pregnant. Red said, "Get her inside and put her on my bed. I started to speak, but Red cut me off, "Yes, my bed, now move," and move I did.

Red grabbed all her belongings she could grab and headed inside. I had her on Red's bed with her feet elevated and wrapped in a blanket. I yelled at Red, "Call Doc and tell him to get here as soon as possible. I don't care if he has to take a dog sled team to get here; get here quickly!" Red called Doc, and after a quick conversation, she told me that Doc had said, "He would have to come by snowmobile, but he would be there as quickly as possible."

Red walked into the bedroom and noticed the dogs on each side of the bed as if they were protecting her. Then, looking up at her, they growled menacingly, and she knew they were protecting her or her and the baby. Why, she didn't know, but she knew her dogs, and she trusted them. She took Joe's hand, led him into the living room, and set him down where he could see if the woman moved one iota. Then she went to the truck and brought the liquor and the groceries she had asked him to buy into the house.

Joe was white as a sheet and also in shock. It was not as bad as the woman and her baby were, but he was in shock, just the same. She poured him a double shot of whiskey and told him to drink it. She poured another and said, "Now sip this one, and when you are ready, tell me what the hell happened?"

I looked at Red and said, "Thanks, but I will be fine. Use some of that alcohol you had me buy and clean and dress the wound on her head to stop the bleeding. She will need stitches, but that will be Doc's job when he arrives."

Red grabbed Joe's first aid kit and the alcohol he bought and did as he said to do. She cleaned and wrapped the wound, and he was right; she was sure it would require stitches. As she finished, she heard a snowmobile pull into the yard. Doc came directly in, went to the patient, closed the door, and went to work.

He knew shock when he saw it and knew they did everything they could do for her with their knowledge. Probably Joe's knowledge, having been in the military, and what they did perhaps saved her, and as he examined her swollen belly, he swore under his breath, "Damn! And on top of being in deep shock, twins." But in the case of a severe concussion, he really could only stitch her up to stop the bleeding. He needed to give her a transfusion, but he didn't know her blood type, so a transfusion was out of the question. Time was the only solution at this point without being at a hospital, which they were far from. With her stitched up and bandaged, he was done.

So, he left the room with the door open, sat down, and told Joe what he had done, which, in his medical opinion, wasn't much. Red watched Doc walk into the living room, brought him a shot of whiskey as well, and he thanked her profusely.

Doc then asked me, "In Heaven's name, Joe, what the hell happened, and who is she? And how she is pregnant, with twins, mind you, with a fully intact hymen, you have got me. Red, I will take one more of these and make it a double. And her room should be much warmer. I want her to be almost, but not quite, sweating."

Then Doc, with a bizarre look on his face, said, "Joe, I want you to know that in all my life, I haven't ever felt an 'aroura' from a person, 'ever,' and she radiates it like a flaming torch.

It was almost overpowering when I touched her near the babies. Can't you see it in the dogs? They feel it, and in their way, they have become primarily those baby's protectors and the mother just a short way behind them. I am not a religious man, but I don't know about this. I don't have a clue." As tears flowed down his face.

I had finished my sipping shot and said, "I want one more, but that is all. And then I will tell you the little that I know and that it is scarce if you really think about it." And boy, did I think about it. *The car, Jesus, I had almost forgotten the car with Dareilene and her dead baby inside her.* Tears rolled slowly down my face as I downed the second shot of whiskey.

Then I told them about topping the rise just before my turnoff and seeing a car across the valley spinning out of control and slamming into what was left of the guardrail. And then, coming upon Mareilene, Mary stood outside of the car and told me her twin sister and unborn child were both dead behind the steering wheel of the vehicle.

After Mary convinced me that Dareilene and her unborn child were dead and the vehicle was on fire and ready to blow, I pushed the car the rest of the way off the cliff into the valley below to hide her from the people pursuing Mary for her baby.

Then we jumped into my truck, and she told me to "Drive like the Devil is on your heels because he is." Then, the longest seven miles in my life were getting her here and trying to keep her from going into deep shock.

And then, crying like a baby, I told them Mary said, "I promise I will explain all of this to you because on this earth right now, God sent you here to save me and, more importantly, my baby. And according to him, you are the only person I and 'He' can trust!" And then I said softly more to myself, "Why me?"

At that moment in the bedroom, Mary opened her eyes and said in a soft voice that everyone could hear for some reason, "God trusts you, Joseph, with his son, and now I know he also trusts you with his daughter. Joseph, we are to be married before the babies are born because they need your name as well as your protection. Your son's name will be Christian Peter Everlasting, 'Christ Everlasting,' and your daughter shall be named Hope Mary Everlasting,

'Hope Everlasting.'"

At this point, Doc went in and, as he came out, said, "She is now resting peacefully; her color is back to normal, and I think she will be just fine. But he goes on, how a woman that was in deep shock only a short while ago, as we all know, and had a severe head laceration is now resting peacefully, I can only say, God only knows, and that I truly mean. As for myself, I am not sure."

As Doc sits back down, Red says, "On that, I am pouring all of us a shot to celebrate life. And life that we all are now tasked to support. We have been tasked with the lives of those three on our own if required. Here is to Christian, Hope, Joseph, and Mary, and all who believe from this day forward. Salute." The three of us drained our respective shot glasses and just sat there, each in deep thought about what had just happened. And how it would change each of our lives forever. I thought to myself, and I was sure the others were thinking along the same line of thought: *God works in mysterious ways.*

I continued thinking, *Damn, we are a strange crew to be in this predicament. And a predicament that only Mary sleeping in the bedroom has any clue what this is all about.*

There's Red, who is a Navajo Squaw and a widow after thirty years of marriage. I never asked if she had any children, and she never brought it up. I guess a subject better be left unknown until she feels like letting me know. I am guessing she was around seventeen when she got married, which put her in her upper forties.

Doc, a black man of Nigerian descent, was adopted as a child by a wealthy, childless couple, who, like my parents, died at an early age when their private plane went down in a severe thunderstorm. He, with his parent's life insurance, put himself through med school and had a promising career ahead of him as he graduated close to the top of his class at Harvard Med School. Instead, he fell in love and married a Dutch woman, Margie, who was a nurse, and moved to the wilds of Colorado to get away from the, as he said it, "the hell of the city" to become a country doctor handling everything medical from delivering babies, to measles and mumps, and even doing his medical magic on the occasional animal if the regional vet wasn't in the area. Doc went directly to med school and then five years of residency. Add on about five years practicing medicine here in Colorado, putting him in his mid-to-upper thirties.

Then there was me, the typical country-boy white kid, who happened to be raised by a preacher and his wife and tended to be a 'bit' rebellious. And just out of spite, I joined the military to piss off my parents. Joining the military helped me grow up and become a man at an early age, which was a good thing.

It was also a choice that I regret to this day because my parents died while I was serving in a special force behind enemy lines in Nam. The military tested me when I joined, and I scored twenty-five above the genius level back in the day. Even in high school, my teachers said that I could have been a straight "A" student if I had even tried. I am thirty, but right now, I feel fifty.

And then there is/was Mareilene, Dareilene, Mary, and Darlene to everybody at school, who were co-valedictorians at graduation. Their parents split shortly after that graduation, with Darlene staying with her dad and attending Fort Lewis College in Durango, studying to be a veterinarian. Mary stayed with her mom, moved to Denver, and attended Colorado Christian University outside of Denver. They were traveling together tonight for some unknown reason when all hell broke loose. Mary is thirty as well, and Darlene, well, she will remain thirty, which is all I can say.

Then, before we could do anything, Mary basically waddled out and sat down in the nearest chair right next to me. Quietly, she said, "Thanks, Joe; without you, the babies would be dead or captured along with me. I owe you mine and their lives, and I will never forget it." And that took almost all the energy she had in her shaking little body, but in her mind, it had to be said. Doc jumped out of his chair and said, "What are you trying to do? Kill yourself and your babies in the process?"

Mary looked at him steadily and said, "You really don't know what this man has done to save not only me and my children but the world itself. Now, if you would be so kind, Doc, please help me back to bed before my watchdogs have a hissy fit."

And if Doc hadn't been there, she would have collapsed right in front of us. Doc yelled at me, "Give me some help!" But I was already moving, and I had her in my arms, moving toward the bedroom before Doc finished his sentence.

As we tucked her into bed, Doc looked at me and said, "You are the one, Joe. You are now the leader. And whether or not you want to be, you are her protector and the man of her life now! I know it is a heavy burden, but I know you are capable of it better than any man alive! Why I feel that way, I don't know, but I know I am right somehow. She is sleeping peacefully, and now I am going to go home. Is it all right if I tell Margie about the events of this monumental night that has unfolded before our very eyes?"

I thought for just a short time, as always, before speaking and said, "Yes, please. She is your rock for your quick thinking, and you make a perfect team. I, no doubt, am going to need all the help I can get, in a multitude of ways, to manage everything coherently. So yes, please tell her everything: your hopes, your fears, your dreams, and mostly your heart. Now go, get some much-needed sleep. Red and I will take shifts to keep an eye on her, but I have a strong feeling she is already in good hands. Do you know what I mean?"

Doc just said, "Yes," and with his head bowed, "Yes, again, I do."

And I continue, "Mark, if I may call you that at this moment, this is a strange time to ask, but Thanksgiving is just a couple of days off, and Red and I would love for you two to join us in a celebration of Thanksgiving like no other."

Mark says, "Margie and I would be honored. See you then, and as Doc again, you call me with anything, do you understand?"

"Yes, I promise," I said. "The snow has let up, but the temp is continuing to drop, so be safe."

As Doc left, I walked out of the bedroom and asked Red, "Do we have at least two shots left in that bottle?" "Yes," said Red, "but that will finish it off."

"Good," I said. "I want to watch her in shifts all night if that is okay with you?"

Red said, "Yes, and that she would take the first shift and would wake me in about three hours. And since it was 4:00 AM, that should be right around seven or so."

I said, "Fine," and took my last shot in one gulp. "We will discuss all this around ten or so in the morning. I will need information to make decisions, and there should be some available by then. And oh, by the way, I invited Doc and Margie for Thanksgiving. I hope that was okay?"

Red said, "Yes, and I am sure there are a few more we need to invite to complete the protection circle if you know what I mean." I shook my head yes as I quietly headed for bed. But before I dropped off to sleep, I asked God for a special prayer of safety for all involved. But before I was completely asleep, I thought, Dad, in your way, you unknowingly prepared me for all of this, and then I was sleeping.

My alarm went off in three hours just as Red was coming to wake me. She said, "No change, sleeping like a baby."

I said, "Snuggle down in my bed. It's warm and ready for sleep."

Red, without any argument, slid in, pulled up the blankets, and was asleep before I left the room. I went to the kitchen and made a fresh pot of strong coffee, grabbed a tablet out of the drawer to make notes of the tasks for tomorrow, no, for today. The two days I had blended into one long, long day. Red had a chair beside her bed already, so I sat down and started to write.

1. Need information about Mary's pursuers, as I thought to myself, pursuers my ass. Joe, it's the Devil.

2. Leave the house using the backway to avoid any questionable people at the crash site.

3. Dress out of character and go out to find information or gossip. The best place to gather information is Jose's Diner.

4. Buy a local and Durango newspaper and scan while basically hiding behind them at the corner end of the counter while reading.

5. Fill up with gas at the north end of town, where the tourists usually fill up and then cruise slowly through town looking for; well, I wasn't sure what, but probably anything out of the ordinary for Cortez.

6. Stop by the grocery store and buy whatever we need for an extended stay at the house. That includes another turkey with more fixings since we anticipate more to attend the holiday meal this year; stop at Pete's gun shop and stock up on all my gauges of ammo, of which I only carried a few. Because the military taught me that a gun without bullets was only a heavy stick, and I finally hit the liquor store.

7. Stop by basically the only real wrecking and tow truck shop in town, Tom's Wreck and Tow, with a cover story about looking for parts

for wind spinners. Such as old side mirrors, bicycle finders, or anything that could be attached to a center axel and spin in the wind. They were used in a garden to keep birds out of it, for example. At least it sounded like an excellent excuse to see if Mary's car was there and if anyone had been there looking it over.

8. Go by the crash site without stopping but checking for suspicious activity, and then continue home again on the back way.

9. Stop at the contractor's office to see if he can have his mason finish his "unique" fireplace before December 1. If possible, write down a description to give to the mason.

I looked at my list and thought Mary, in her concussive state, said we were going to be married. Taking that statement as faith, drop off my parents' wedding rings to have them cleaned because, well, because in Mary's condition, not to mention everything else, the option of going and picking out rings was out of the question.

As I finished, Mary stirred and opened her eyes, looked at me, and said, "I knew you would be here watching over me," then rolled over and was back asleep within seconds. I drafted the ideas I had for the fireplace in my room (I am going to have to work on 'our' room) so as not to take up too much time in town with my contractor friend, if he was even in his office.

Red got up around seven, got a cup of coffee, and then walked in to check on me and the patient. I motioned for her to go into the living room and showed her my list. Red looked through it and said, "I'll make a quick list right now. I know you want to get going. But first, I have a few questions that nagged me while I babysat."

"Go ahead," I said. Red thinks about where to start, and then she says, "You know, the fewer people that know Mary and the children-to-be are here, the better, right?"

I said, "Yes, I have already thought of that, and they will have to be people like Doc, who really need to know. Speaking of which, one of us needs to tell him Mary and the babies are fine and to keep this all to themselves. I told Doc that only those that need to know get to know. At least, that is what I think I said. Everything is still sorting itself out at this point. In fact, I will give him a call right now to let him know about Mary and the babies and to ensure the secrecy of all this."

I dial Doc, who answers immediately and says, "I can guess what two things you are calling about. The first is Mary and the kids, which I figured are fine. Otherwise, I would have heard from you long before now and the other. No one else is to know a thing, which is except Margie, and I trust her with my life. I'm right, aren't I?"

I say, "Yes, I knew I liked you for some reason. That's all, except you guys are coming for Turkey Day, right, say around noonish or so?"

Doc says, "Wouldn't miss it for all the 'Tea in China.'"

I hang up, look at Red, and ask, "Noonish is okay, right?"

Red says, "Noonish is okay. I will give Margie a call later and let her know what to bring."

I say, "Okay, back to your questions."

Red then goes on, "So the list that knows should be small, has been covered, and probably Doc and Margie will put together a potential list, at least to start with, of people that should be in the know. Next, your trip into town will probably answer a lot of questions, but Joe, I am worried about all of this like you wouldn't believe. When Mary said, 'Drive like the devil is on your heels,' I have a strong feeling that wasn't a metaphor. And I really think she meant the . . . Devil! Joe, we can't fight the devil! We might have to make a run for it." But taking a deep breath to calm herself, she said, "I think your trip into town today will clear up our plans. I wouldn't say I like it, but I don't see any other choice. Luckily, I think yesterday's storm gave us cover for at least a little while. Later, when Mary wakes up, she can fill us in on all we don't know. But I think what we do know is only the tip of the iceberg. Until then, all we can do is pray that you get at least some of the answers that we need this morning. So go get changed, grab a gun and extra magazines out of your 'hidden' gun safe, and head into town like now."

I shook my head and said, "How did you know?"

Red just rolled her eyes, went back to her grocery list, and said, "How many men that you know have a closet that big, even if they are married? And that is another thing we have to discuss in detail when you get back." I said, "December 1 will be the day because something, or someone, is telling me that Mary will be in labor on December 24, and the twins will be born late on the twenty-fourth or early morning on the twenty-fifth."

CHAPTER THREE

I quickly headed for my bedroom, went to my 'hidden' gun safe end of the closet, and pulled out my 9mm handgun with five extra magazines to be on the safe side. I looked at my clothes and decided on just a laid-back weekend look since, well, it was the weekend. I had a sweater and leather jacket to hide that I was carrying, blue jeans, and a pair of hiking boots, just in case I ended up in the woods for some unknown reason. And if I was on foot in the woods, heaven forbid, it was because nothing good was going my way at the time.

I walked out and asked Red, "Do I look incognito?"

Red said, "Did you mean, 'Do you look like a dork'? Yes, but it will work for the weekend."

"Just what I thought, not the dork part, but the rest. I guess good minds think alike. Can you see my gun?"

Red looked me up and down and said, "No, not unless I knew it was there, but no one will suspect."

I said, "Thanks, and you have the list right in front of me so that I won't forget it. Smart thinking. I will be back; well, I am not sure when, but hopefully well before dark. That back road is a bit tricky in the dark."

Well, as I headed north instead of the typical south to the main highway, I noticed to the west a line of very dark storm clouds that would probably be in the Cortez area about midafternoon at the latest. Which meant the back road would be trickier the longer I was in town.

It had been a while since I had been on the back road, and I was sure that the last storm had really torn it up.

It would not only be tough after dark; it might damn well be impossible, especially if the storm had heavy snow in store for the mountains. So, I tried my best to make good time, but I had to pull out the chainsaw twice to get around downed trees. I chopped up the trees and stacked the wood in the back of my truck for two reasons. One, it made me look like I had been out getting firewood if needed as a cover story later. Second, the weight would give me much-needed traction if I needed it. Then I reached the highway, and if you didn't know the back road was there, you'd never see it.

As I drove toward Cortez, a wrecker was working to get the car out of the valley and almost had it to the edge of the cliff. The good news was that it was from Tom's, but the bad news was that there were two cop cars and, more interestingly, a black Suburban with what looked like Delaware plates. I made a mental note of the plate numbers and went on without even slowing. I headed for Jose's Diner, grabbed the two papers I wanted, sat down at the end of the counter, and ordered coffee. The waiter was a new guy, so no problem with him. The story on the cover of each paper was the same. Each addressed the car crash over the cliff, but with only scant details except that the remains of the body of a pregnant woman had been recovered, but no identification had been made at that time. I thought, *Well, I knew that much. But that was just the preliminary investigation. By now, the wreck was on top, and the cops were looking a lot closer than the EMTs would have. So now it was time to listen and see if anyone had seen anything of interest and was discussing it with their friends. That is when I got my first tidbit of info.*

Three guys, all dressed in black, got out of a black Suburban and came into the diner. I could see three of the license plate numbers on the Suburban, but those three were the last three of the plates on the Suburban at the crash site. They sat in a back booth, with two vaguely watching the door while the other had his back to me. And strangely, they shed their overcoats like they were roasting. Everyone else in the place still had their coats on because even though they were inside, with the door opening and closing, it was a bit chilly in the diner.

Although it didn't really make sense, I would have sworn that none of their feet touched the floor. Not just one of them, but all three of them. They weren't small men. So, their feet did not touch the floor, and it had nothing to do with their size. They all ordered black coffee with six coffees to go. Within a minute or so, they had drunk their coffee, paid, and were leaving. And I know the coffee at Jose's. It is served boiling. Jose thinks it keeps the patrons there longer, so they will order a more extensive breakfast. Who knows about Jose? He is a very strange critter himself. Drinking that hot coffee, like iced coffee, only added to their uniqueness.

I paid and slowly followed them out, and luckily, I was parked in front of them. And to add to everything else, the plates matched the Suburban up on the hill.

Cortez is a small town with basically one main street going east to west and another highway on the west side going north to south. So, following too close was dangerous. As I sat in my truck, they pulled away from the curb and headed west. I was able to follow at a discrete distance without being noticed. They continued west upon leaving the diner, and at the intersection of the two highways, they turned north. Then, within a few blocks, they turned left into the parking lot of the last motel in town. And there, to my wondering eyes, would I see, but two more Suburbans with Delaware plates, with five men, again all dressed in black.

I thought to myself. *Obviously, they really didn't care about sticking out at all in this small town, and they were loading luggage. All except one man, who exited the room as I was turning north onto the highway. He walked over to the last and the bigger of the Suburbans and took a seat to himself in the back. Just looking at him made me involuntarily shiver. He carried himself like a Prince. A person who lets ordinary people do the work. Not because he didn't want to, but more because it was below him, way below him!*

Then, when they were done loading the luggage, they all loaded up and headed north toward Monticello, Utah. The road continued through Moab and then onto Interstate 70. Since the road is basically a two-lane highway, following them was out of the question. But I bet myself ten bucks when they hit the Interstate; they were headed east. As I pulled into the gas station, I noticed the 'For Sale' signs being stuck in the ground in front of the motel and the gas station. No, no connection, at least that I could think of.

As I filled up my truck, I pulled out my checklist. I still had to stop at the contractor's office, the jewelers, the liquor store, the grocery store, Tom's Towing, and the gun shop, not necessarily in that order. And then home, still using the back way because I wasn't at all sure I accounted for all of the 'Men in Black.'

Then, just as I was getting ready to get back in my truck and pull out of the gas station, a young man exited the Prince's room, but he was dressed in typical garb for this time of year in Cortez. But what was he doing in that room?

Then, to buy some time, I raised the hood to check the oil. For once, I actually did because I was usually not one to check my oil level regularly. Then, the young man started walking east toward downtown.

For some reason, he looked familiar to me. Then, like a light bulb above my head, it came to me. He was the new waiter at Jose's that I had dismissed as 'inconsequential.' So all the 'Men in Black' were heading north. Or were they? Had they left a very ordinary-looking young man in their midst to be a spy?

And where would he gather any information of any concern to the Prince? The same place where I had gone to gather information and gossip was Jose's. So, I was right. The 'Men in Black' made a big show of leaving town on purpose. I was now sure they did because they left an insurance policy behind. The Prince was anything but dumb. Counting Jose's new waiter, there were at least one, if not more; moles still holed up in Cortez. They would be hidden in plain sight, being the eyes and ears of the Prince. At least for a while, to make sure that he hadn't missed some minor detail that could make a difference between a dead savior and a savior who is alive and well. I was sure that he thought all was accounted for, but as the military has taught me, never count on anything, no matter how small a thing it might be. And now I know. If I ever meet up with him again, remember. He thinks like I do.

I could see the Prince in the back of the Suburban smiling to himself. The asshole! I decided in the near future to make my presence known at the diner and have coffee with the other guys looking for work, just to be expected and to keep an eye on their spy. The next stop was my friend, the contractor, and as luck would have it, he was working on his books when he was usually closed this time of year. I knocked on the door, and my friend Ralph opened up and said, "What brings you here this late in the year?"

I said, "Remember that fireplace? I wanted it to be unique. I need it done before December 1st. Do you think your mason can do it?"

Ralph says, "This time of year, I am sure he will 'make time' to do it." "Good," I say. I have what I want on paper here, but I will give you a quick rundown if you have a few minutes."

Ralph said, "Sure, go for it."

I said, "Okay, the concrete backing is already built in a semi-circular design. It's sort of like an old-time baker's oven. The body of the fireplace I want is made of dark gray flagstone. To make it different, I want the flagstone set at an angle and on the edge. The opening to the fireplace is circular, with the exception of the very base. Around the circular opening, I want the stone mason to place alternating long and short white marble in the shape of a sun with dark gray flagstone worked in around the curved shape, in between the white marble.

For the lower mantel, I want a blood-red, curved piece of flagstone to represent a sunset, with black flagstone laid horizontally and on the edge below the red flagstone to the floor. The upper mantel, built of a single piece of black granite, would curve around the chimney. Two smaller suns with polished brass centers will be stacked on top of each other going up the chimney, which will be all black flagstone except the suns.

Ralph loved the idea and said, "My mason is a fireplace genius. And unless something unexpected pops up, he should be able to do it easily before the first."

After seeing Ralph and making all the other stops I needed to make, except Tom's, I had some information. But not much, if you didn't count the Prince, the Men in Black, or minions, as I decided to call them, and obviously the waiter, a minion in his own right.

The only other clue that came up was at Tom's. One of Tom's guys was going through the wreck and found an ID behind the back seat that was only partially burned. And it had Mary's name on it, but that was about all. I told Tom he had better call the cops and tell them what they had found.

Tom called right away, and the Cortez police sent a cruiser over in minutes, bagged the evidence, and said, "Thanks a lot! Until this ID was discovered, we really knew very little about the woman, except that she was pregnant and attended school near Denver due to a partial school sticker on the bumper." I hung around long enough to make sure the cops got the clue and then told Tom, "I found a few things that I want and have set them aside, but this storm is already starting to snow, and I will be back next week to do some more looking."

Tom looked at the sky and said, "Good luck; this looks like a doozie of a storm, and getting home isn't going to be easy." I headed home at a good clip, and as I was driving, I thought, Tom, if you only knew how I was getting home, he would have wondered why, and even if he didn't, he would have thought I was crazy.

As I approached my turnoff, I checked out the crash site, and it was quiet. But again, that didn't mean anything in this day of sensors, cameras, and all other sorts of remote sensing equipment that could transmit via satellite worldwide if you paid enough.

I only got stuck once, but I used my wench and was back going forward in about fifteen minutes. I got home about twenty minutes after total darkness, and Red was beside herself! "What in the name of God took you so long? You have been gone for hours," said Red.

I just looked at her, smiled, and said, "It was worth it, at least I think it was. I'll tell you all about it over a nice shot, or maybe several shots!

Wait, how is Mary?" Red, with a look of how stupid a man could be, said, "Look at me and multiply times ten, and you might, and I mean just might be close to how worried she is about you. You would think you two are already married. And just so you know, mister smarty pants, she totally agrees with the dates and your reasons. Now I will have to live with you being right about 'that' forever as well."

Then she kissed me smack on my lips, hugged me like I had been gone forever, and said, "I give thanks to God with all of my heart, mind, and soul that you are all right. Now, let's grab everything out of the truck and bring it into the house. This snow is coming down hard, and it is only going to get worse. And you have shots to drink and a story to tell two very worried but now very thankful women."

As I walked back into the house, Mary wrapped herself around me, as well as a very pregnant woman could. Then she said, "I will never let you out of my sight again. And then she added, so help me God. I wouldn't say I liked worrying about you second by second, minute by minute, and then long agonizing hour by hour, which turned into hours. And then the darkness!"

And she continued, "When you told Red your goal was to be home, well before dark! And you out chasing the Devil himself, what am I going to do with you?" She looked at me, confused about which to be. Angry as hell or so happy that I was okay that she could break down in tears. She picked the second option and sobbed uncontrollably with her arms around my neck, and I just stood there feeling so bad that I cried with her. She finally stopped and said, "What you put me, no us through, better be damn, well worth it, or I won't even speak to you until I say, 'I do.' You got it, mister; I didn't choose you. Well, I did secretly in high school, but that doesn't count; God picked you!"

I looked at her and asked, "You wanted to marry me in high school?"

Mary said, "Forget I ever said that, and I mean it. If you ever bring it . . ." She couldn't finish her statement because I was kissing her like she was the only woman in the world to me. Which, in my mind now, she was and always would be. I, in my heart of hearts, knew. One day, I will die, saving her and the children. The thought scared me but also brought solace, knowing what I was now meant to do and that I would do it without hesitation.

Then Red walked up and said, "Now that all the mushy stuff is over with, here is your shot, and you had better have earned it, or it will be a tranquil house with both women in it not speaking to you! Now sit down and let us know about your day, 'sweetheart.'" Mary was beside herself laughing at Red, but the laughter died as I started with the trip down the back road and told them just how bad it was after last winter. And that I had to use my chainsaw twice to get to the main highway. I outlined what was happening at the crash site with the cops, Tom's wrecker, and the black Suburban with the Delaware plates. Then I told them about Jose's and that a new guy was working behind the counter, so he was hidden in plain sight. And then I told them about the three guys in black and all their strange quirks, for lack of a better word.

At that point, Mary pulled her blanket tighter around herself and the babies and said, "Just you talking about those three scares me to my core. And, Joe, you know me from way back, and I'm not a scaredy-cat, but?"

I said, "I know. Let's say they got my attention and then some, and it gets even creepier if that is possible." Then I told them about tailing the three of them as they left the diner, and sure enough, they got into the same Suburban I spotted at the crash site. And then I said, "Well, I tailed them in my truck to their motel, and that is where it really gets weird if it isn't weird enough already."

There were two other Suburbans with Delaware plates loading up luggage, but the next-to-last man out of the room really got my attention. He was also all dressed in black, but something about him screamed, this is the "main man"! He walked with a purpose. Just his demeanor said, 'I am the Prince, and all others are nothing, nothing at all, except to be used.'

So, from that point on, I thought of him as the Prince. And the more I think about it, the 'Prince of Darkness' fits him perfectly!

I look at Mary, who is as white as a sheet. And I say, "Mary, do you mind if I sit beside you on the couch?"

Mary, with tears in her eyes, just shook her head yes and said, "Oh yes, please, Joe. What you're saying is scaring the living bejesus out of me. And bring your blanket. I know it is warm in here, but I'm so cold."

I looked over at Red and asked, "Red, would you please bring me another? I think I need some warming up as well, and I have more to tell,"

"No problem, Joe," said Red. "I could use some warming as well before you continue."

As Red was getting a couple more shots to warm them both up, I got up, grabbed my blanket, and spread it over Mary. Then I sat down, scooted over beside her, and wrapped up in the blanket as well.

Red came back with two brimming full shot glasses. And then she clicked glasses with me and said, "Glad you're home, salute!" Both glasses were empty and on the coffee table. And once Red was down and comfortable, I began again,

"And then, once the minions had loaded everything, they started up and headed north toward Monticello and Moab, which eventually meets Interstate 70. As both of you know, that interstate heads toward California or the East Coast. My educated guess would be that they went east toward Delaware. At this point, I had my tank of gas full as planned. I was going back to my truck door when you would never guess who walked out of the Prince's room."

I looked at both of them before I said, "The new waiter at Jose's. They may have left town, but they all didn't, if you know what I mean." If it was possible, Mary snuggled even closer. I told them the rest of the stops were inconsequential, with the exception of Tom's towing.

I said, "While I was at Tom's, pretending to be looking for junk parts to make wind spinners out of . . ." Red asked, "What a wind spinner was?"

And I thought, *Good girl, Red, get her mind off of the bad and onto something totally different.* I said, "A wind spinner is to keep birds out of your garden. They are built on an upright pole, usually three or four cups per level, which face opposite directions on each of four or so levels, and they catch the wind and spin, hence the name, wind spinner. Easy to make."

Red says, "I'll take five, one for each corner of my garden and one for the middle. The fence keeps the deer and critters out, but the birds wreak havoc with the vegetables, especially my tomatoes."

Mary gives Red a big smile, knowing what she is doing by changing the subject. So I continued, "While I was at Tom's, one of his workers found a partially burned ID with Mary's name on it and showed it to Tom and me. I told Tom to call the cops right away.

"Tom called and told them that they had found some evidence in the burnt-out car that had been brought in that they definitely would be interested in."

With the police station only a few blocks away, a squad car was there in just a few minutes. The patrolman said, "Thanks. Until now, we have been in the dark about who the pregnant woman was."

I continued my story by saying, "My good deed for the day was done, and since the weather had taken a strong turn for the worse with the snow coming down hard, it was past time to hightail it out of town and get home. Then I finished up with my getting stuck on the back road and having to wench myself out, and then I was home. At the end of my story, ladies, it is sad but oh so true." I did say one more thing about the trip, though. I said, "I'll be going back to Jose's to have coffee with the other men looking for work, just like I usually do. Not that I'm keeping an eye on the waiter; there's nothing at all like that, mind you!

Then I looked over at Red and asked, "So, Ms. Red, did I hear you say I was right about something? Now, what was it? Oh yes, dates." The pillow hit me square in the head before I even saw it coming.

And then, very solemnly, I got up off the couch and went down onto one knee. I pulled a small box out of my pocket, opened it up, and said, "Mary Johnson, would you make me the proudest man ever and marry me?"

Then Mary, in her finest theatrical voice, said, "Why, Mr. Everlasting, how could any young maiden turn such a fine man as yourself down! And as she put her hand out and I slid the ring on her finger, she cried, "Yes, Joe, you crazy fool, YES! I am yours, my love."

And I thought, *'Till death do us part,' but even then, I know, yes, I know, I will always be at your side, my love. God said I was to be your protector, and I always trust God to know what he is doing.*

"Now, ladies, is there at least a scrap of bread this poor soul could have to eat? It has been a long time since, well, I am not sure of the last time I ate, but all of a sudden, my stomach says it has been a very long time," I said. "And Red, since you are so good with that bottle, may this same poor soul please have another?"

Red rolled her eyes and asked Mary, "Do you think he earned another?"

"Well, this time, I guess it is okay, but I am watching you, Joe. And by the time you really get to know me, you'll swear that I have eyes in the back of my head. Mark my words, mister," said Mary.

It was a simple dinner of leftovers, but to a man as hungry as I was, it was a meal; as I looked over at my wife-to-be and looked down at her stomach, I thought, *fit for a king, not any damned Prince!*

It had been a long day for everyone, and the ladies turned in as soon as the kitchen was cleaned. But before Mary turned in, she stopped, came back to me, sat in my lap, put her arms around my neck, and said to me very softly, "Good night, my love. I know why God put you back in my life, and I am beyond happy! And then, with tears flowing down her cheeks, she continued, 'I know it is a burden no ordinary man could carry, only you, and I will love you beyond the 'Till death do us part,' I hope you know and believe that."

I held her as if I never wanted to let go because I didn't, and the only thing I could say was, "Ditto, baby! Now, get to bed; you need your rest. I am going to stay up just a while longer. Love you!"

As she got up and went to bed, I stared at the fireplace and thought about what she had just said: 'Till death do us part,' and I looked up toward heaven. I got up, went to bed, and said a prayer, which wasn't my usual. Sleep took me, and peace washed over my household and me.

We all went to church the following day, which again wasn't normal, but as things went on, it just felt, well, right. Plus, I wanted to talk to Fr. John privately, and right after the service, it seemed like a perfect time.

Fr. John, Fr. John Paul Polo, to be exact. Fr. John always said he was named after John Paul II since the first John Paul died only thirty-three days after he became pope. People of the parish called him their renegade Catholic since he started in Rome at the Vatican, basically as a lowly priest who traveled the countryside preaching at small churches.

To him, doing that was just a bit of heaven on earth. But what he couldn't really stand was the politics of Vatican life. He finally left Italy for the United States and ended up in a big Catholic church on the east side of New York City, which was just as political, if not even more so, than the Vatican, where he had just left. After a year or so, he headed west and ended up in the 'Wilds of Colorado,' where he finally put down roots. He started a small church that was slowly but steadily growing.

Funny, I thought, I never really thought of Colorado as the end of the earth, but I guess for a lot of people, it is. And to them, it is 'Heaven on Earth.' To me, it was just home, but now it seems it might just be as they think, 'Heaven on Earth.'

As the service ended, I told Mary I was going to talk to Fr. John for a minute about coming to Thanksgiving dinner if he was available. Mary looked at me with a 'what are you doing?' look and said, "I'll be in the truck. Don't be long."

"I won't be," I said.

Then I walked over to Fr. John, and I asked, "Fr. John, do you have a minute?"

"Sure, Joe," said Fr. John. "It's not often I see you in church, not to mention in the presence of a pregnant young woman. What can I do for you, or is it more what can God do for you?"

I think about my response for a second and then say, "Well, a couple of things, Father. First, I, or I should say we, would like you to come to Thanksgiving dinner, and secondly . . ."

"Go ahead, Joe."

"Okay," I said, "I am getting married on the first, and if you could, would you marry Mary and me?"

Fr. John just said without hesitation, "I would love to come for dinner, and I would be honored to marry you."

"We will fill you in on the details on Thursday. Everyone else, which isn't many, will be there around noon. Could you be there, say, eleven or so?" I asked. Fr. John looked at Mary getting into the truck and said, "I have a powerful feeling that there is a lot more to this story, but I will wait to hear it."

"Thanks," I said. "See you around eleven on Thursday."

"Should I bring anything?" asked Fr. John. "No, I think the ladies have everything covered," I said as I turned and walked to the truck.

As I jumped into my truck, Red said, "That was a long invite to Thanksgiving. Don't you think so, Mary?" I just shook my head and said, "Women, I can't live with them; I can't live without them. What's a man supposed to do?"

And they both burst into full-fledged belly laughs.

CHAPTER FOUR

Well, we all got back from church and had a bite to eat. Mary patted her tummy and said, "We are going to take a nap. Besides being one heck of a week, I think I might be pregnant. What do you guys think?"

Red burst out laughing and said, "Well, maybe; what do you think, Joe?"

As I look her up and down with a big smile on my face, I say, "Could be, but I am just a man; what would I know?"

And Red, laughing even harder, said, "Yeah, you're right, what would you know?"

Mary says, "Very funny, both of you! I'll see you in a couple of hours. I'm going to try to sleep if you guys can keep quiet out here."

Red says, "We'll try," and almost falls out of her chair. "Come on, Joe, let's see what game is on, and we will be quiet so the little woman can sleep."

The game was a blowout, so I asked Red if she wanted to take a walk. Red said, "Yes, either that or I am going to take a nap as well." So, we took off and left a note for Mary, just in case she got up and got worried about us and headed up the road to the north.

And, of course, Red asks, "So what did you and the father talk about?"

I said, "I figured you would get to that sooner or later. Well, if you must know, besides asking him to dinner, I asked him to marry Mary and me on the first." Red goes, "You did, didn't you?"

"Yes," I said. We have to have it official, and he is the only one I can trust around here.

So, what do you think?"

"I think it is a great idea. Nothing else?" asked Red.

"Did you know that a southwest wind like this usually means a storm is approaching?" I said with a solemn voice, as I just barely missed getting hit in the arm.

"You know what I mean," said Red sarcastically.

"Oh, you mean Mary?" I asked.

"Yes, Mary!" said Red.

So, I go on and say, "Well, if you must know, no, I didn't mention Mary, but I did ask him to come to dinner about eleven instead of noon. I said we had a few things to 'talk' about."

As Red stops and rolls her eyes, I continue, "He said, 'He figured as much' and said he would be here at eleven.' Do you feel better now?" I asked.

"Yes, and I expect we will have a white Thanksgiving if you must know," said Red as I slapped her on the ass. Then she said, "Good thing Mary wasn't here to see that, mister or you would be in big trouble." We both laughed, turned around, and headed home.

When we got back, Mary had just gotten up and asked, "So what were you two talking about now? I could hear you laughing all the way down here."

Red thinks for a minute and says, "The weather." We both burst into laughter again, much to Mary's dismay. So, after we stopped laughing, I told her what we had been discussing. She was glad to hear that Fr. John was going to make it for Thanksgiving and that he was going to marry us. But she was not so pleased that he was coming an hour or so earlier to discuss a few 'things.'

"Joe," Mary said, "but he is a priest and well."

And I said, "Yes, he is a priest. He also said that he had a strong feeling that there was a lot more to this wedding than just being pregnant. He didn't say that exactly, but I could tell he knew we would tell him what was up when he got here. And we left it at that. Okay?"

"Okay, but try to break it to him easily. Promise me." Said Mary.

"I promise and swear to God. Oh wait, should I put my hand on..."

Both Mary and Red go, "Joseph," and then I wondered aloud, "Did you know we just might have a white Thanksgiving Day? I'm hungry, and I am sure the horses are too; I'll be back in a while," I said. And, as I backed out the front door so I could dodge a pillow if one were coming my way, I could hear them both still laughing.

As I came back in, dinner was on the table, and a new game was on. At least this one looked close. During the meal, I said, "I have a stone mason coming to the house tomorrow morning to start work on the fireplace in my bedroom. He will just be taking some measurements since he was the one who cast the bare concrete fireplace I have now, and he has a few questions about my 'unique' design for the fronting of it. He will start the work on Tuesday.

And Mary says, "Well, what is it going to look like, or is that a 'big' secret?"

I said, "Well, my dear wife-to-be, it is 'my' bedroom, and it is 'my' secret until I decide to tell you or we get married and you move in. One way or the other, you will know, but not until I tell you or we are married."

And now I said, "To totally change the subject, I think after the mason leaves, I will go into town tomorrow." And in unison, I get a loud, "Why?"

After a long, drawn-out period of silence, I continued as I was about to say. "I was going into town to pick up a pie at the bakery to take to my friend's house for Thanksgiving after I stopped at Jose's to have coffee and check on the new guy. That's why."

Mary thinks for a minute, and I can tell Red is probably thinking along the same lines. So I answered before asking, "It is always better to know what your enemy is up to at all times, and if I can lead him off track, even somewhat, the better it will be for us."

Red goes, "I don't like it, but I have to admit it does make sense. As long as it is a short trip, got it?"

I said, "Got it, but I may stop at the little bar on the north end of town to have a beer, just to make sure I am not being followed. If I am, I will take a little longer to get home and stop at Jim's because I can make it look like I live there. Since I always walk right in and get a beer out of his fridge. And he asks, "What's up?"

I continue, "So you have it all. Plan A and plan B if needed. Besides, I want to establish the north route home as well, just in case we need it. Do I have your blessings, ladies?" Mary says, "Okay, but no matter what, make it quick."

I said, "Believe me, I can get here multiple ways from Jim's. That is why I picked his place to start with. And he has a hidden camera out front, so he knows who is coming a quarter of a mile away."

Red goes, "Well, even if he is a man, I guess his military training paid off, at least somewhat."

Mary looks at me and says, "You will be leaving early, right?"

I replied somewhat sarcastically, "Yes, Mother. You would think I am already married." And simultaneously, as they had practiced it, they both stuck out their tongues at me.

Margie was coming over tomorrow, so that they would be busy with Thanksgiving and wedding preparations. They wouldn't dwell on me all the time, but still, most of it. So I would be up and out around seven or so. The bakery was to the west of Jose's, so if I had a tail, I should know pretty quickly. Especially since it was Thanksgiving week and most of the town's businesses would be closed, or so I hoped.

I rolled out of bed around 6:30 a.m. and headed for the kitchen, made a pot of coffee, and as I waited for the coffee to brew, I thought about my upcoming trip to Cortez. *After my shower and a cup or so of coffee and a thermos to go, I would head out the north route to the west road into the north end of town. Then I would go south and turn east on Main and make a U-turn in front of Jose's if the traffic was light or a left into the gas station, fill up again, and then park just to the west of Jose's. Go in, grab a paper, and have a cup of coffee. It should go smoothly, but you never know.*

Mary came into the kitchen about the same time as I was pouring a cup and said to me, "Joe, go ahead and pour two more. I heard Red stirring around, and she should be out here in a few."

I poured three cups and took all three to the coffee table by the couch where Mary was sitting. I handed her a cup and sat down with mine as she said, "I see you are up early as promised. I was hoping you would be. It wouldn't be seemly for me to be rolling you out of bed, especially since at this point. I don't know how you sleep. Do you know what I mean?" And I said, "Pajama bottoms so that you know."

"Morning all," said Red as she came out of her room.

"Good, you are up early and made coffee, good man. We might keep you around after all. What do you think, Mary?"

Mary looked me up and down and said, "He will do, at least for the time being. So, Joe, give us a quick outline of your plan for the morning, and you do get the emphasis on the morning plan, right?" I was tempted to answer, 'Yes, Mother,' but thought twice and figured I should give them the plan.

"Okay. Head into town via the north route, head to Jose's, make a U-turn, park just to the west, get coffee and a paper, and check out the 'new guy' situation. Then, after that is established, I head to the bakery and pick up a pie, continue west, and then head north, watching out for a tail. At that point, if tailed, plan B kicks in, and I stop for a beer and wait to see if the tail continues north; wait a while, then I head for Jim's. If the tail is still 'tailing me,' I pretend I live there and ascertain if the tail remains or figures I am home and head back into town or wait a while for the tail to leave. Then, continue home to the two most beautiful women in the world. What do you think?"

Red and Mary look at each other, and Red says, "I don't know about the 'beautiful' part, but other than that, it works for us. Right, Mary?"

"Right, but call if you have any deviation, and I do mean any deviation, Joe!" Mary said.

I said, "Got it." and headed for the shower.

Dressed in a light jacket, shirt, jeans, and boots, I grabbed my thermos of coffee and headed for the door. On the way out, I kissed Mary on the cheek as I passed her and said, "Don't worry. I will be back in one piece. Remember, God has a job for me to protect you, and this is part of it." "I know. Just be safe, Okay?" said Mary.

"I will check my six all the time. I don't trust these 'men in black' any farther than I can throw them, which wouldn't be far. Most of them are pretty big guys. See you in a while. Bye and love you!" As I left, I thought, I sure hope it will be a short and not a long time.

I jumped in the truck and headed north. The good thing about pickup trucks is that everybody drives them, and with the red clay on the dirt roads, you can't even tell what color the pickup is unless you are right beside it: Colorado camouflage. The weather was warm ahead of the front rolling in, and the skies were clear; a perfect November day in southwestern Colorado.

I got into town as planned and was able to make the U-turn right in front of the diner since the traffic was even lighter than I anticipated. I walked into Jose's to find out I was the only customer. That would present its problems. I grabbed a newspaper and ordered coffee, hoping to remain somewhat discreet, but no luck. The waiter walked up and said, "Didn't I see you in here the other day?"

I said, "Yeah, I have coffee here all the time, especially during work-finding time. It's pretty empty in here. I guess most left town for Thanksgiving."

The waiter says, "By the way, my name is Felix. What's yours? I take it you live around here." *Felix the Black Cat,*" I think to myself as I reply. "My name's Joe, and I live about five miles northeast of here. "So, Felix," I say, "what brings you to a little town in southwestern Colorado during the start of winter?"

"Well, Joe, I'll get your coffee, and I'll tell you when I get back unless you are in a hurry to get somewhere?"

"No, coffee sounds good right now," I said, and as he left, I thought, *as usual, nothing you plan works out like you intended. Remember, Joe, keep it general, nothing specific.* Here's your coffee. If I remember, you like it black, right?" said Felix.

"Right," I said as I took a sip. "It's just as hot as Jose makes it. So Felix, what brings you to the 'Wilds of Colorado,' as they say?"

Felix cocks his head as if thinking, *what should I say?*" and then says, "Well, I was hitchhiking across the country, and it was slow going. As winter was approaching, I came into Cortez, and as I passed Jose's, there was a 'Help wanted' sign in his window, so I went in and got the job. Then, I found a small apartment at an excellent price and thought, 'Looks like I am here, at least for the winter.' How about you?"

I said, "Born in the Midwest, my parents died, headed west, and ended up here. Well, thanks for the coffee; it hit the spot. Here's a couple of bucks, so keep the change for rent. I have been invited out of town for Thanksgiving, so I am stopping by the bakery on my way out of town to buy a pie. You've got to take something, and since I am not the best cook in the world, a bakery pie will have to do. I am not sure when I will be leaving, but it will be before the traffic headed north gets heavy on Wednesday. Well, I have to get going. I got horses to feed. Take it easy and enjoy turkey day!"

"Thanks. See you when you get back, but in case I decide to move on, it was nice meeting you," said Felix.

And I think as I walk out of the diner and jump into my truck, *Okay, Felix. You come into town, get a job at Jose's, and rent an apartment, and you 'might' decide to move on. Obviously, it's a very fluid situation you're living in.*

Then, I took a quick look in the rearview mirror, and right on cue, I saw Felix putting a 'Be back in an Hour' sign in the window. Signaling, I will have a tail. Plan B kicks in, and it is still early, which is okay for the ladies back home. And really, it wouldn't be the first time I had a beer at nine in the morning, hasn't everyone? No, Joe, everyone hasn't!

As I head for the bakery, a black pickup pulls slowly out of Jose's back parking lot. Do all those men in black drive black vehicles, and did his story of his hitchhiking across the country go out the window?

And the pickup just washed and waxed from its looks. I mean, if you're going to tail anyone, try to blend in at least a little bit. I thought. *What the hell did they teach you in devil school, anyway?*

I walked out of the bakery, headed west, and took the turn to the north, as planned. And the black truck with Felix in it did the same. And I'll bet he didn't anticipate I would stop at the bar. I am pretty sure he was underage. So, for him to go in was out of the question, so he was in a bit of a pickle.

As I entered the bar, I sat where I could see out the window, and the black truck slowly drove by and then continued north. It seems like he might wait up the road somewhere unless he gets tired of waiting. So I ordered another light beer; it was 3.2 percent alcohol beer, so two definitely wouldn't impair my driving one iota. Especially with all the coffee I had drank and the bowl of chips and salsa I just finished. I figured I had been there, say, at least a half hour or so. So now I shall see how determined Felix is. I jumped in my truck, took a side road north and another back east, stopped at Jim's, and shot the shit for a while And if it presented itself as the right time, give him some, only some of my dealings in town.

I pulled into Jim's in about twenty minutes and parked right in his garage, which luckily was open. Then I walked up to the front door just as a black truck came slowly rolling by. How he knew, unless it was the dirt from the road kicking up, I didn't know, but it bothered me. And then I walked in as if I lived there, making sure that Felix or maybe another 'minion' saw me enter.

Jim says, "I take it your entrance was to ensure the tail in the black truck knows you 'live here.' And as you get a beer, bring me one as well."

"Your wish is my command," I said. "I knew you would see me coming, and if anyone were behind me, you would know that as well. And Jim, I have a serious question for you! Do you believe in the 'Devil'?"

Jim sat quietly and sipped his beer before he answered. Then he said, "Before I answer that, tell me why you are asking the question, especially as strange as it is."

Now, I was the quiet one, and I was thinking, *How much can I say? I trusted him with my life, and in Nam, he saved it. So, not everything by any means, and I will tell him that, but it is just what he needs to know now.* So I said, "Okay, Jim, you know me, and I don't say anything unless I have facts to back it up, right?".

"Proceed," said Jim. I took a deep breath and said it plain and simple, "The Devil and his minions are in Cortez and have been here since that car went over the cliff with a pregnant woman inside.

The Devil recently left Cortez but has left some of his minions behind to make sure all is as he was assured, and the woman and baby found dead east of Cortez are the ones he was searching for. So Cortez, at the moment, is now a 'little piece of hell on earth.'"

I go on, "The Devil believes; no, I think he thinks he knows, that the woman was carrying the second coming of a savior."

"Damn," said Jim. "How do you know all this?"

So I said, "It is a very long story, and I promise to tell you every bit of it in detail in a very short time. Let's say I saw the Devil, the 'Prince of Darkness,' as he is more often referred to. So, without further explanation, and that I am not at liberty to say at this point, I am here because I needed a place where I knew that I could act like it was my own. And sorry to say, your place fits my plan B perfectly."

Then Jim says, "Great, now we are fighting the devils' minions in Cortez. What next? A forty-year flood. Jesus, Joe, what are we doing this for?"

"The only thing I can say is I have been tasked with protecting a mother and her baby and saving the world. It's a piece of cake, wouldn't you say?

And Jim, with that arsenal that you have, if needed, I think you can take care of any minions that might come this way. Now, the actual devil, I am not sure anyone but God himself can do that," I said.

Jim goes, "Wait, here comes the black truck back again, and it's going at regular speed. I guess he figures you are here for the long run. By the way, how long are you staying?"

"Just long enough to allow him to get back to town, especially since he hung a sign in the window of Jose's saying he would be back in about an hour, and we are over that time already. So I'll wait ten more minutes or so and then continue on home, making sure your garage is closed when I leave. And just so you know, his name is Felix, and he is Jose's new waiter."

"Great," said Jim. It's the only coffee shop in town where I actually like the coffee."

"I also told him I was headed out of town to visit friends and would be gone for a while. So I don't anticipate you having any visitors. If you do, tell anyone you are just house-sitting,"

Jim said. "House-sitting my own house. That should be easy enough," he said with a smile. I will be waiting for more Intel on this later, got it?"

"Yes," I said as I headed out for my truck. I pulled out of the garage, shut the door, and honked goodbye to Jim as I pulled out of the driveway. I then continued east. I was at home just after noon.

The women were ecstatic and wanted to hear everything, but Mary said, "They were in the middle of a big project and would be done in a couple of hours or so. And to have a shot or two, just as a reward for getting home on time, 'this' time."

I said, "Fine, I have a call to make to a friend in Idaho anyway, and it will take some time. You ladies, by all means, go about your 'women's work.'

I got three glares, which I followed up with, "which I know is very important." And if I hadn't moved quickly enough, I would have been hit with a pair of scissors as they flew across the room in my direction. I went and poured myself a half shot, drank it, poured a full one, and headed for the phone in the living room.

As I sat down in my chair by the phone and the fireplace and started to make a call to another old Nam buddy, I thought about what I was going to say. I knew he and his wife lived in Idaho as survivalists, so I figured his place might be a good choice if we needed a 'Get out of Dodge' quick plan. At least, I hoped. Anyway, I figured you can't count on anything in a predicament like ours, and I am sure we will be in it for the long haul.

As I started to redial his number, I stopped and thought about my decision to bring him into the fold. Frank's real name was Francis; his mother was a Catholic, but after Nam, he said he just wasn't sure if he believed anymore.

Nam did that to a lot of men, especially if you were in the bush, not knowing if the next bullet had your name on it. But of all the people in the world, not counting the present company, I trusted him more than anyone else to cover my six. Even if it meant taking a bullet to do it, with that said, I dialed. The phone rang four times, and I hung up. Again, I dialed, and the phone rang four times and hung up again. I waited for two minutes and dialed again and heard Frank's distinctive voice saying, "This had better be good."

I said, "Frank, it's Joe. How are you and the wife doing?"

"Damn, Joe, I thought you had died or something. I haven't heard from you in a couple of years, to say the least," said Frank.

"Well, Francis," I said.

Frank goes, "You asshole, I told you I would kill you if you called me that again! Good thing you are on the phone!" And I heard him laughing in the background, which I knew he would, and it would lighten up the conversation we were about to have. "Okay, I promise, never again! I need to talk to you if you have the time," I said to Frank.

"Yeah, I am all ears," said Frank.

"Well, are you coming down this way for Thanksgiving?" I asked.

Frank said, "Yeah, we leave tomorrow for Farmington, and we will be there for a couple of days or so afterward so the wife can catch up with some of her friends. Why do you ask?"

I said, "Well, I thought you might stop by for a few days with your wife; what is her name?" "Lucy," said Frank.

"That's right, so Lucy, your wife, will get to meet Mary, my wife-to-be," I said.

Frank almost choked and said, "The man that said he would never get married, is?"

"Yes, everyone changes, look at you. We could drink a few beers and talk about the good times that we had in Nam," I said.

Frank goes, "The 'good' times, or the 'excellent' times?"

I said, "The 'excellent' times, if you know what I mean."

"I got it," he said. What's a good time to drop by? And can we stay for a day or so if you have room? I am sure we have a lot of 'excellent' times to talk about."

I said, "Sure, and if you would be so kind, I do sort of need a best man as well. And in this special case, it is essential to have a best friend to be my guy at my side."

"I see. First of all, yes, I would be honored. When is the wedding?" asked Frank. "It's the first of December, a Wednesday," I said. Frank said, "Consider it done. We will be there on Sunday afternoon. That will give us some time to let the ladies do their thing and let us do ours. Is that a deal?"

I said, "Works for me like you would not believe. So how is the family? I understand you have a little boy now. What's his name?"

Frank says, "Funny, you should ask, and it was Lucy's idea, so don't get mushy on me. But she likes the name, Joseph, being the Christian she is, but we call him Joe."

I said, "Imagine that. I had a feeling I picked the exactly right person for best man, not to mention other things. See you three on Sunday before the wedding, and thanks!"

As I hung up the phone, I thought about Thanksgiving dinner. Then I thought about Fr. John and figured I had better call him and suggest an earlier time since this is going to be quite a shock to a priest, especially a Catholic priest. I dialed his number, and he answered within a couple of rings and said, "Hello, this is Fr. John. May I help you?"

And I said, "Fr. John, this is Joe. After some careful thought, I think maybe an hour and a half earlier might be better. We have several things to discuss, and we will need your opinion on many of them. Does that work for your day?"

Fr. John says, "I have an early service on Thanksgiving morning, but I should be able to make it. See you then. I have a feeling this' discussion' should be more than a little bit interesting. Talk to you then."

With that done, I finished my shot, walked into the kitchen, and checked on what the ladies were doing. It looked like they were finishing up, so I said, "Well, I have a best man lined up, and he will be here with his wife and kid on Monday afternoon before the wedding, so we will have to figure out the sleeping arrangements soon. His name is Francis, but do not call him that; he goes by Frank, and he will kill me if he knows you know. His wife is Lucy, and his son is Joseph, Joe for short. He is an old friend of mine from Nam. And I also talked to Fr. John, and he agreed to come about an hour and a half before the others to discuss the issues we want to talk about to get his opinion. Mary started to say something but stopped. I was thankful I got through that news without being shot. So, I had a glass of wine instead.

CHAPTER FIVE

Thanksgiving Day was tomorrow, and the kitchen was not a place for any man to intrude upon except to get a cup of coffee or a beer. I knew my life of drinking, which really wasn't much at all until that night, which seems so long ago, would very soon change back. So I grabbed a beer and a shot.

I checked on the mason, and he was making excellent progress. It was already coming together even better than I expected. I told him to shut it down and go home, and I would see him after Thanksgiving Day if that worked for him. He said, "It did, so we were set, but he would be busy Saturday and Sunday. He would be back on Monday and was pretty sure he could finish up by then."

I said, "Well, have a great Thanksgiving."

Looking back at his work, he asked, "Are you sure?"

I said, "Yes, see you Monday."

Then I went and sat down and watched the game. Which I had to say was really good. But as I sat, I thought, Just how long had it been since that night? With God as my witness, I couldn't tell you if my life depended on it. I am going to have to look at a calendar and then make some notes for the future. In fact, I should be writing all this down for the children once they're of age to understand. I suspect it will be much sooner than we all think. I don't know why; it's just a feeling, I guess. A strong feeling if anyone really wanted to know.

As I said, the game was good, and it ended when Margie left. Red and Mary flopped down on the couch, exhausted, especially Mary. This was to be expected, with her carrying twins and all. I asked her if she would like a small glass of wine. We both looked at Red, and she said, "A small one would not hurt at all."

So I got up and got it for her, and she just smiled a big smile and sipped slowly, making every sip count. Red then said, "We will have to figure out our decision on the sleeping arrangements for your best man and family, but that can wait."

"So, how did the morning go? Just because we were up to our asses at work didn't mean we weren't wondering and worrying all the time. But first, I want to thank God you made it home on time. I really couldn't believe it when I heard your truck pull up. So spill it, or do you need something to 'loosen up your tongue'? And you know, all those habits, which we both have been partaking of, will be part of the past," said Red.

And I said, "Yes, Mother Red." And I also said, "Yes to your first question. As for the second, I have already had that discussion with myself and have come to the same conclusion. Some occasionally, but not like the last few days? How long has it really been since all this started? I tried to remember, but I can't. We need to sit down and start a diary of events after Thanksgiving and keep it going from now on. Agreed?"

Both Red and Mary said, "Agreed."

Mary said, "It is too important to the children, and you know what, to the world if you really want to know. Damn, is that a sobering thought or what. But instead, let us now dwell on the present. Red, get your drinks; I want to hear what my 'husband-to-be' has to say about his day."

"Did you know it is going to snow tomorrow night?" I said with a smile, and everyone laughed. Red brought the drinks, and I began my story.

"Well," I started, "it all went according to plan except for the fact that I was the only one in the diner. The town was all but deserted. It seems most of the people in town decided to hit the road before the snowstorm hit the road. Anyway, I grabbed a newspaper and ordered coffee. The first thing the waiter said was, "I saw you in here the other day."

"So much for being anonymous," I told the ladies.

Then he said, "My name is Felix. What's yours, and where do you live?"

Again, I told the ladies my thoughts were "Felix the 'Black Cat,' and secondly, that I had to change the subject to him as soon as possible. So I said, "My name is Joe. I come in here all the time with the other guys looking for work. And I live to the northeast, about five miles or so."

"So, Felix, what brings you to Cortez?"

Felix said, "Well, I am hitchhiking across the country with winter just around the corner. As I was walking down the street, I saw the Help Wanted sign in Jose's window.

Felix then said, "This town is as good as any. So I went in, got the job, and found a place to live, and it looks like I will be here for the winter."

I downed my coffee and said, "Nice to meet you, but I have to go. I have to stop at the bakery and get a pie. I'm going to a friend's house for Thanksgiving, and I have to bring something. And I'll be there for a while, not much in the way of work, going on with winter right around the corner."

And then he said, "Have a safe trip. I might decide to leave; who knows? It was nice meeting you in case I don't see you again." With that, I left and headed for my truck. But in my mirror, I watched as he put a sign in the door window that said, "Be back in an Hour."

At that point, I knew my tail was beginning. As I drove away, a black pickup pulled out from behind Jose's, and the tail was on. I went west and then north as planned and stopped at the bar, guessing he wouldn't be old enough to come in.

I stayed there for about a half hour after he slowly drove past the bar heading north. Then I got into my truck and drove north as well. I took a different route to Jim's, which required an additional left and then a right to make sure I lost him.

But as I was pulling into Jim's, I spotted him about a quarter of a mile back. I am guessing it was the dust my tires put into the air, which alerted him to my location since he knew I said I lived about five miles to the northeast.

Then I told the ladies that it bothered me more than a little that, with all my turns and such, he 'knew' where I was. Anyway, then I pulled into Jim's garage and went right in, making sure he saw me go in without knocking first."

As I walked in, Jim said, "I take it you intended to make your tail think you live here."

I said, "Yes," as I took a beer from his fridge, brought him a fresh one, and sat down beside him in another chair.

Then I told him, "The story about the 'Devil being in Cortez,' and how it was a 'little piece of hell' now. I filled him in on a few more facts about how I knew this to be accurate and that the person driving the truck was one of his minions. I also told him he was working at Jose's, which he didn't take well at all because the diner was his favorite place to have coffee in the morning with all the locals. In addition, I told Jim that I was pretty sure, not 100 percent, that the minion's name that was driving the black truck was Felix if he cared to know.

I also told Jim, "I told Felix I was going out of town so that I wouldn't be around for a while."

"Good," said Jim. Then I told Jim, "Felix told me that if I didn't see him again, it was nice meeting me since he might be leaving sooner than he thought."

Within minutes of that part of the conversation, Felix came driving back in the black pickup toward town at a decent speed. I said to Jim, "He is probably driving that fast because the sign he hung on the door at Jose's said, 'He would be gone around an hour.'"

I waited for about ten more minutes, and before I left, I promised Jim that I would fill him in on all the details later.

And then, I came straight home and got the cold shoulder from all of you. Really, I am just kidding; I know how much work goes into an everyday meal, and this is a Thanksgiving meal, for heaven's sake. So, it seems to have worked out. But I am just not sure anymore. I am

99 percent sure, but I wish I were 100 percent sure. But as they say, 'Beggars can't be choosers.'

And speaking of beggars, what can I have for a snack? I am starving. It seems like yesterday was the last time I ate; wait, it was. Never mind, you two worked your tails off today. I'm sure after being a bachelor for as long as I have been, I can find something to eat without messing up your meal."

As I made my sandwich and the girls went to bed early since it had been a long day for them as well, I thought, *What if it hadn't gone right today, and I had made a mistake in going to check on who I know now is Felix. It seems as if I live almost every minute of every day now with 'what ifs.'*

And if I think about it, I don't think it is going to change much from now on. And on top of everything else, tomorrow is Thanksgiving! At this point, I wish it was already Thanksgiving Eve. Because tomorrow is going to be a day that will definitely go into our notes, or should I call it our 'Journal of Life' from now on?

I looked down at my almost-finished sandwich, took the last bite, and headed to bed after what I can only say was, 'One Helluva day in the 'Wilds of Colorado.'

Well, the day finally arrived, and Mary was a nervous wreck! Not about the meal and all, but about the impending visit of Fr. John. Then I thought, *Joe, change the subject, and that I did.*

"Mary," I said, "would you like to know a little bit more about my best man?"

And she goes, "I've been meaning to ask you about that, but something else always comes up, and it slips my mind, so tell me why Frank, or Francis, as you say we are never supposed to mention, why him?"

Well, now that I had brought up the subject, I had to have an answer, and I said, "Frank was a friend, a 'very' good friend of mine in Nam, as I told you. And Frank and Lucy, I think I told you she was Catholic, right?"

"Yes," said Mary. "Please go on."

"Well," I said, "Frank and Lucy live up in the 'wilds of Idaho.' It's not like what the people around here call the 'Wilds of Colorado.' I mean, they really live out in the extreme sticks. Miles from any place you could call civilization. They're essentially survivalists. They are self-sustained and have a thriving community of families, with some singles but mostly families."

I stopped for a moment to sip wine, taking it easy since it was going to be a long day. And I knew I had her attention when she said, "So what does this have to do with anything going on right now?"

"Well, to get to the point," I said, "I figured if we ever needed to get the hell out of here and have a place to go, Frank's place sounds like a perfect destination. So, ladies, you included Red because where we go, you are coming, hopefully?" I said rather thoughtfully.

Mary said, "Well, I hadn't ever thought about it, but it makes sense to have a plan B if needed, as you say. A place like that would be a great place to disappear. What do you think, Red? Oh, and before you answer, you will be coming with us, no 'Ands, Ifs, or Buts' about it. Understand!"

"Yes, Mary. Under no circumstances would I not!" said Red. And I said, "I am going to tell Frank, and I am confident he will tell Lucy all about the goings on here with you and Cortez's unexpected 'guests.' I figured he would make an excellent addition to our 'circle of protectors,' COPs for short, for you and the kids."

Red goes, "You know, one day, you just might make a good husband for some fine young woman."

"Well, what do you know, Fr. John just pulled up," I said. *So much for the distraction, but it worked for a while,* I thought.

Mary turned slightly pale as she looked at the door and thought, *Be brave; he has to know sometime, and now is as good a time as any.* And then there was the knock at the door, and Red opened it and said, "A good Thanksgiving Day to you, Fr. John. How did your service go this morning?"

"It is Red, right? Thanks for asking. It went well, but with everyone home cooking, the turnout was not what I hoped. It was good anyway that people came and gave thanks to the Lord," said Fr. John.

"And this must be Mary, nice to meet you," and as he took her hand, Fr. John exclaimed, "'Mary, Mother of Jesus'!" And he let go of her hand and knelt, crossed himself, and quietly said again, "Mary, mother of Jesus?"

Mary took a deep breath and calmly said, "No, Fr. John, Mary, mother of Christian Peter Everlasting, and Hope Mary Everlasting, soon to be. And then in the future, to be known as Christ Everlasting and Hope Everlasting. And, Red, will you get the father a glass of wine? I think he needs one at this moment. And I am sure a second glass may be needed soon. Now, Father, please get up off of the floor and sit down."

Fr. John crossed himself again and said, "Mary, you are not just carrying the coming savior, but his sister as well?"

At that point, Mary looks at me, then Red, and finally at Fr. John and says, "Father, this is going to come as a very, very big shock, but I have it on good authority, 'as she looks toward Heaven,' that they are, shall we say, both Saviors."

Fr. John, whose religious faith has just been shattered, says in a single statement more to himself and God than anyone else in the room: "Two saviors?"

He paused for several minutes, handed his empty glass to Red, and said, "To the rim, please." And again, more to himself and God, he says, "I had a strong feeling, but not this damn strong! Forgive me, God, please. It is your will!"

And then, turning to look in my direction, he sternly asked, "Joseph, why! Why in God's name? May he be blessed forever. Didn't you tell me this?"

"Well," I said, "to be blunt, I have been pretty busy fighting off the 'Prince of Darkness' by myself."

Fr. John crosses himself yet again and says, "You actually mean the 'Devil,' don't you?"

"Yes," I said, "not to mention all his minions. I have been, you could say, pretty busy for at least the last three weeks or so. And not to change the subject, but Red, I think the father will take that second glass of wine now. And as requested, pour it to the rim." "Coming up, Father," said Red.

I look at Red and point to my empty wine glass, and she says, "I get the hint, Joseph."

Fr. John looks at Mary and says, "Okay, so let me get this straight. Mary, you are pregnant with twins, and one is a boy and one a girl, and they are both from God. Am I right so far?"

"Yes, Father," said Mary. And Fr. John goes on, "How do you know you are carrying the saviors? Named Christian and Hope, 'and I am sure we will hear that part of the story later,' but he asks again. How do you know?"

Mary took a deep breath and said, "An angel came to me one night and told me God had blessed me, and he had chosen me to be the mother, as the Virgin Mary, before me was."

At this point, Red exclaims, "What angel? We haven't heard that part of the story!"

Mary says, "That's because we were busy with you know who, really up until yesterday. And I just have never had time to get to that part of the story. Sorry, guys."

"Now, back to my story," said Mary. "The angel left, and I was speechless. I figured I must be dreaming, or hallucinating or . . . or something. This couldn't be possible. I was, and still am, a virgin, although you wouldn't know it from looking at me. I even went and got one of those pregnancy tests, and yup, I was pregnant. And if it hadn't been for the accident and Doc fixing me up, I wouldn't have even known I was going to have twins."

Mary continues, "And here is the naming part of the story, Fr. John. When I was in the throes of deep shock, I told Doc, Joseph, and Red the children's names and that Joseph and I were going to be married, and he was going to be their father and protector. And this was all according to what God said to me."

Mary continued again, "Joe will fill you in later on 'All' the details of the last few weeks, and believe me, it will make your hair stand on end. Joe has been a hero to me and the children. Now you know at least the highlights of my story. Joe will be the one to fill you in on the rest because he is the only one who can. He has been on the front line for so long that between the three of us, we really are not sure of when all 'Hell' actually broke loose."

"Red, I will take my glass of wine now, and I will have another during dinner, and God help the soul who tries to stop me," said Mary.

I held up my empty wine glass and two fingers to ensure that Red realized I still wanted wine, not a shot of whiskey.

Fr. John just sat there slowly, sipping his second glass of wine, and let all this slowly sink in. Finally, he said, "Joe, I want to hear every detail of your dealings with 'you know who' and how you actually survived.

Then, looking again at Mary, still awed at . . . at just about everything and reverently asked, And if, at all possible, I would be blessed to be at birth Mary, if you would allow it? I would forever consider it the most incredible day of my life! And if possible, again, I would love to be a part of the children's lives for the rest of mine, so help me God."

Mary says, "You are welcome to be here on Christmas when they will be born. You can keep Joe company while he waits."

Fr. John swallows and says, "You know they will be born on Christmas Day?"

"Yes," said Mary. "I will go into labor on Christmas Eve, and 'they' will be born shortly after midnight. And again, I have it on good authority." The Fr. shows Red his empty glass, and she obliges him.

"Now, Red," says Fr. John as he takes a deep breath to control himself, "I understand you and Mary are quite the cooks, and might you have an appetizer available? I think this wine is going to my head, and I am just so happy to be here for this Thanksgiving! And what a Thanksgiving it will be! It will be etched in my mind forever. Especially on December 1, when you two, Joseph and Mary, wed, and I will perform the ceremony. Heaven can only wait until I can tell this story to the world. Amen!" And the rest of us echo, "Amen" as well.

So, about that time, the other guests started arriving, and a great Thanksgiving Day it was, as most if not all, knew of the significance of this day and the upcoming births. The meal was outstanding from beginning to end. The ladies of the house and those who brought their contributions to the meal went beyond what a typical Thanksgiving meal would be. To say it was magnificent was an understatement! And all the wine didn't hurt at all. But the most memorable thing was just before the last guest left, who was Fr. John.

Mary was in front of the fireplace, standing there thinking, *Well, that was one fantastic Thanksgiving from beginning to end. Thanks, Lord.* Then, Fr. John walked up to her and solemnly kneeled in front of her. And Mary said, "Father, what are . . .?"

Fr. John looks up and asks, "Please, Mary, bless me! I have waited for this moment for all my life, as all people who believe do."

Fr. John continues in an almost trance-like way and says, "We, all of us here, are at the threshold of an event which will change the world in a very different way than most people would, or even will, at first believe.

Then, taking a calming breath asked,

"Mary, if you would, please 'Bless me'?"

Mary looked at me, and I shook my head, 'Yes.' She put one hand on her stomach, felt two kicks, and smiled, knowing somehow that they 'Knew' and blessed it. Then the other hand on his bowed head and said, "In the name of the Father, Son, and Holy Ghost, may this man be blessed. Amen!" And Fr. John openly wept and, through his tears of solemn joy, said,

"Thank you from the bottom of this sinner's heart, and 'May God keep you and guide you through your trials.' Amen!" He then got up quietly and left the three of us alone, as he opened the door and walked out a changed man.

Then I walked over to Mary and said, "Take a sip as I toast. To Fr. John, a man who truly walks with God tonight." Mary took her sip, and I finished her glass as the snow began to fall in earnest outside of the cabin. And then I said, "I know Mary can't join us, but Red, on this august occasion, would you be willing to partake of a hearty shot of whiskey with me?"

Red smiled through her tears and said, "I would be honored, sir." She poured two, we clicked our shot glasses, and we both shot them down. Then we both sat down, me beside Mary and Red in the chair by the fire. Everyone seemed to take a deep breath as we relaxed and discussed the day from start to finish. And what a day it had been. We sat quietly after that as the fire died down. Then Red and I did a fast cleanup of the last of the stuff out on the counter, and each of us went to bed with our private thoughts on the day.

The next day looked like a winter wonderland, with the fresh snow blanketing everything. And there on the windowsill was a pair of pinion jays, eating seeds laid out by Red for their Thanksgiving meal. Red was enjoying them as always and said, "I guess all the excitement of the dinner kept them away. But they are enjoying the sun and their breakfast after Thanksgiving Day, whether they knew it or not." For us, coffee, muffins, and pie from Thanksgiving made for a great breakfast sitting by the fire.

After a quick cleanup of our breakfast, I told the ladies, "I fed the animals and cleaned the stalls early this morning, so no chores at this point, so I am going on a hike to clear my mind,"

"We'll go with you," they both said, and I said, "Sorry, but no. I am going up to the point, and it will take snowshoes to get there, even if I can make it on them." "Why?" said Mary.

"Well," I said, "after yesterday and all that happened, and don't get me wrong, it was amazing. Then you add in the few weeks prior to yesterday, put them both together, and I need a little 'me' time if you know what I mean."

Without speaking, they both just nodded their heads yes as I continued, "There is this rock point on the west ridge where I, for no better reason other than it's where I go, to talk to God. And I need a little talking right now."

So I go to the closet, where I keep my snowshoes. I keep them there just in case the snow is too deep to get to the barn to feed the livestock on intense snow days.

As I was getting the snowshoes, I thought I needed to check the fences from above while I was up to the point. It was much easier than walking the fence line in snowshoes. And besides, I need to exercise as much as I need the time to myself.

I say, "So you two relax and take care of the fort while I am gone. The weather is great, and I should be back in an hour or two. As long as God isn't too long-winded, which he tends to be at times, and now, it just might be one of those times."

So I got my lighter jacket because snowshoeing is hard work. Grabbed a backpack, a couple of bottles of water, and one of Red's rolls, said "Bye" to the ladies, went outside, strapped on the snowshoes, and headed west toward the ridge.

The going is easy at first, but as soon as I get to the base of the ridge, I have to start switch-backing up the ridge following sort of a trail. I stopped halfway up and grabbed a good swig of water. A distinct and needed change from wine and whiskey, which is good because soon, water will be the mainstay, and liquor a pleasant reward. Then I looked back east toward the house and was proud of what I had accomplished over the time I owned the property, which didn't even have a house on it when I bought it.

Then I thought, No time to be patting yourself on the back when you are only halfway to the point, and the rough part is still ahead! So I put the water bottle back in the pack and headed back to the task of getting to my rock on the point of the ridge. If it had been summer, it would have been a piece of cake, but in winter and on snowshoes, it was a different story. Time flew by, and after wiping the snow off, I was sitting on my favorite rock, enjoying the quiet sounds and the beauty that only nature can deliver if you really think about it.

As I was checking out the fence lines for any problems, and luckily, none were noted, a black truck came into view and was headed toward my house. I jumped to my feet, ready to take off down the hill at breakneck speed, when I realized it was an old pickup; Ralph Jones, who lived about six miles up the road, was just headed home. *Damn*, I thought, *Joe, you are wound as tight as a clock spring. Relax, that is why you are up here.*

I took a deep breath and pulled out that roll that Red made. And took a bite. As I chewed it, a thought crossed my mind: *That woman can make a dinner roll to die for, generally speaking, in these precarious times. So, it was time for what I actually came to do! Talk to God as if that was so easy. Well, it always had been, but now? The general conversation with God, which I basically had with myself and which gave me a feeling of peace and, more importantly, a sense of not being alone, had taken a decisive turn from general to urgent. Well, as I continued to think, okay, go for it.*

Looking up, I said out loud, as I always did, "Okay, God, I have one significant question, that question is not why me? My real question is, why, or in other words, how do you know this is going to work?

I do not really doubt you, but I have read Revelation, albeit quite a while ago, and the scholars, whoever they might be, interpreted your words as saying that you had sent several saviors. They didn't bother to say what happened to them, but God, several are more than just a few. And if you don't mind me asking, what, and excuse my French, what the hell is different this time than with the others?

"Joseph!" I jumped to my feet and looked around. I was sure that I hadn't been followed. The voice said again, "Joseph, it is different because the Savior is different. The Savior is Saviors. Don't you see?"

And I say, "God, is that really you talking to me?"

"Yes, Joseph, it is 'I'! And I am trying to answer your question. Can't you see the children, the saviors, hidden in plain sight? Do you think it was just a 'coincidence' that Christian Peter, 'Christ,' and Hope Mary, 'Hope,' were to be born together as brother and sister? Think about it, my son. The searchers for a savior are looking for the wrong thing, so to speak.

They are looking for a potential savior, not a pair of saviors. Christian will have hope because of his sister Hope. Hope will be there as his equal in times of dire need. When everything that you and Mary have done for the fate of this world is slipping away, she will be his only hope."

"God," I say, "I am sorry, but I still don't understand. Remember, I am just the man you chose to marry Mary and to be the protector of her children."

"Joseph, I understand, so please just listen to me, okay?" said God.

I said, "I am sorry. It isn't every day that I 'actually' talk to you. Please forgive me and go on."

God says, "No, forgiveness is warranted or expected of you, Joseph. Hope is going to be there when he needs hope more than anything else. That is why I sent her to be a savior in her own right. Joseph, I have great faith in you. You are doing well, better than I expected, with all of Hell coming down on you, and I am very proud of you. You have taken on a burden that would have dwarfed almost all men. You think before acting, but when instantaneous events require instantaneous action, you react. 'Plain and Simple'! But what makes your reactions correct is something intangible inside you that makes you who you are. Always trust your instincts, my son, because, more often than not, they are right.

By sending two saviors, I have given you the ultimate advantage… Time. Time to plan, time to learn your enemy, time to become who I know you can be, and finally, time to execute methods from mundane to extreme to do 'what must be done.'"

God continues, "And you, my son, as much as I hurt to say it, you are correct in the fact that you will die in saving the three of them: Christ, Hope, and Mary. Mary will die after helping you in your final task and when she sacrifices herself, as she saves Christ, Hope, and ultimately the world. She will be with you, my son.

"But please don't despair. I know you have already accepted your death, and what you don't know is that Mary has done the same. But what I want both of you to know is that you can tell her. Is that in the final battle, you will both be back for the 'end.' And even though I am God, the 'end' has yet to be determined. It depends on you and your duel with the Devil.

Mary will be a small but pivotal part of the duel as well if that makes sense. But you, you will be the deciding factor. Mary will aid at a time when you need it most. But you and your wits and faith will make or break the outcome. And now, as I go, I will part with this . . . As Mary and Red would both say, 'Got it'?"

And then, God was gone. The quiet of the forest was gone, replaced with nature's song as if nothing at all had just happened.

I sat down on my rock, swallowed hard as I ate the last of the roll, and reflected on what had just happened. Yes, I said I was going to talk to God, but heaven be with me: He just spoke with me!

As I sat there contemplating, I thought of something I read in boot camp, which seems so long ago right now. It was written by a young man named if I remember right, Martin Treptow, who was fighting in France in 1917 and was killed carrying a message between battalions under heavy artillery fire. On his body, they found his diary, and in it was written, and I will never forget this part: "America must win this war. Therefore, I will work, I will save, I will sacrifice, I will endure, and I will fight cheerfully and do my utmost as if the issue of the whole struggle depended on me alone." At that point, I realized it wasn't America; it was the world. And it wasn't Martin, it was me.

I worked my way down the ridge slowly, yes, because it was dangerous, but also because I just needed some time. Time to let what happened sink into my brain and, more importantly, into the very deepest depths of my heart.

Then a pleasant thought crossed my mind: If only Fr. John had been there. I think he would be on his way to heaven right now. I took a deep cleansing breath, smiled all the rest of the way back home, and said out loud to really no one, "Wait until Mary and Red hear what happened! And that God actually said, not me thinking he said it, he said it out loud, exactly what they would have said to me. They will die."

As I walked into the house, smiling like The Cheshire Cat, I said, "Red, a big shot for both of us and Mary, a nice glass of wine. And then you two had better both sit-down.

Now, whether or not you two believe it, God actually just talked to me." I paused to let this sink in. And then I continued. "Not in my head, mind you. He talked to me like I guess he talked to Moses. No burning bush or anything like that. He just talked to me. More importantly, he told me why Christian has hope. God said, 'There will come a time when Christian is totally without hope, and Hope will be there to give it to him. That's why he sent two babies, both saviors, in their own right.'

And what is so crazy? As I was sitting on my rock waiting, I remembered reading the Book of Revelation, which says that besides Jesus, God has sent several other saviors and that they all died, one way or another. Therefore, God said to me that without Hope to give

Christian 'hope,' when he is totally without any, there wasn't any hope for this Savior either; makes sense to me."

"There is more to tell that I need to tell Mary in private. Red, I will fill you in later, I promise. Is it a deal, Red?" "Deal, Joe," said Red.

Then I said, "Red, please bring another round for all of us."

Red goes and gets the shots and wine and serves them on a silver platter because somehow she knows this is something more than just the usual. And I say as I raise my glass, "This isn't sacrilegious, but it is a toast to God. Red and Mary looked at each other, crossed themselves, and we all said, "To God!"

Then Mary says, "Well, it sounds like you had a fascinating conversation, to say the least, and I can't wait to hear what you are going to tell me in private, but I will wait patiently because, for some reason, I know I must."

I said, "I think I need another one to say, 'loosen' my tongue. Red, if you would be so kind."

Red, with a bottle in hand, poured me another shot, and I sat down in my easy chair and started my story about my journey up the ridge and the pleasure of just being alone. The quiet and the workout were a pleasure. And then, while I was on top, I spotted a black truck coming toward the house, and I panicked until I figured out it was actually the neighbor from about six miles up the road. At that point, I then realized just how strung out I was.

That is when God entered my conversation with me, which I have already described somewhat in detail.

But God did say one other thing at the end of our conversation that should actually let you two know that it happened, as I said.

God said the following: "And now as I go, I will part with this . . . As Mary and Red would both say, 'Got it?'" And then he was gone.

Red and Mary were amazed that God spoke their names and knew what they would say. But then, when they both thought about what I said about the other saviors in relation, Hope and hope, they looked at each other, joined together in a quiet hug, and wept unabashedly.

As they finally parted and dried their eyes, Mary said to me, "You, my husband-to-be, are truly a man of God's heart."

CHAPTER SIX

On Monday morning, the stone mason, Johnny, came out of the bedroom and came over to me as I was drinking my coffee, plain and just taking it easy. He said very quietly, "The fireplace is finished, and if I may say so, it is one, if not the best works of 'art' I have ever done, as God is my witness. As soon as I clean up a few more things, you can show the fireplace to the ladies. But no fires until, say, Friday evening, as I want to make sure all the stone is set to last a lifetime."

I said, "No fires until Friday evening, and even then, keep it small! Perfect timing, Johnny. Here is your pay and a 25 percent bonus. I am sure it will come in handy with Christmas just around the corner."

Johnny says, "Thanks, Joe, you didn't have to do that. The fireplace was a work of pure love. And Joe, I would so appreciate it if I could come by someday soon to take a few pictures with a fire going. You have my word that the pictures would be just for me and my family. You know you didn't have to pay me the bonus, but I am so sure that our Christmas will be special because of it. Thanks again. And since I won't see you again for a while, God Bless, Merry Christmas, and congratulations on your upcoming wedding."

Johnny was finished and out of the house in about twenty minutes, and I said to Red and Mary, "There is something I would love to show the two of you if you would be interested?"

Mary says softly, "It is finished?"

I said, "No more perfect words could have been spoken. Please walk to the bedroom with me."

As they entered the bedroom, they each stopped and stared. And Mary said, "With a fire, it will be Father, 'Son,' and the two 'Saviors' in the nighttime sky waiting to be born."

"That's my vision exactly," I said. Red just crossed herself and said, "Between your vision and a stone mason from heaven, you two created a masterpiece where a fireplace should be."

And Red goes on, "I know we have all been good lately, but this, this deserves a shot, maybe two, as she smiled at me, and a glass of wine."

Mary said, "Two and a large wine."

So Red went and got the fixings, and we drank and just admired the "artwork" in front of us.

As the days flew by, the wedding was soon on the horizon. Frank, Lucy, and Little Joe pulled in on Monday at about 3:30. Mary and Red were busy in the spare room working on what I assumed was the wedding gown, especially since I was sworn not to enter that room upon pain of death. Lucy asked, "Where are the ladies working?"

I just pointed to the only shut door in the house. She walked over to it, knocked, and was pulled right through. " It must be nice," I said under my breath.

Frank and Little Joe walked in carrying all the bags, and I said, "Put them over by that door. Frank, you and Lucy get that room, and sorry, Little Joe, you get the couch."

Little Joe says, "Fine by me. I have been on a couch since we got to Farmington. There is nothing new here, Mr. Everlasting."

"Just call me Joe, and for now, you will be Little Joe. Is that okay with you?" I asked.

"Yes, Sir. Little Joe, but only for the weekend. Deal?" Little Joe said as he held out his hand.

"Frank, there is cold beer in the fridge, or if you would like a shot, it is in the cabinet above the sink. And if you do have one, make it two. I feel like a pariah in my own house, if you know what I mean. Tell you what, I feel like a shot with a beer chaser. Are you in?" I asked.

"Well, it has been a long drive from Farmington. I think it was about an hour and a half, and that road can be 'tough,' so yeah, I'm with you. How's the game?" asked Frank. "Really not bad. And Little Joe. There is soda or cold water in the fridge if you are thirsty," I said.

At that point, the ladies came out all laughing at something obviously funny to them, and as Mary walked over to Frank and Little Joe, she introduced herself and said, "As you can probably tell, I am Mary, the bride-to-be. I'll bet you would have never guessed, right?"

Frank said, "Not in a million years. Nice to meet you, and here is what we call Little Joe to keep things straight if you know what I mean. We wouldn't want you to be marrying the wrong man."

"Dad," said Little Joe, "that was just more than a little rude!"

Frank said, "Fine, Little Joe, Mary, (as he got down on one knee),' I apologize for my rude comment."

Mary, pretending to be somewhat dissatisfied, says in a very pretentious way, "Just don't let it happen again," and she and the other ladies burst into laughter. "And now for dinner, ladies. We have a couple of guests coming over tonight for a special celebration, so we need to get to it."

I look at Frank, and he shrugs his shoulders as if to say, 'I have no idea.' Then, I looked over at Mary and asked, "What celebration?"

Mary goes, "Did I say celebration? No, I think you are right; I think I did. Now, you know Joe, when a woman is pregnant and going to get married, very soon, I might add, they get, say, a little forgetful.

Now, let me think. Oh yes! Well, since the road is snowed in and there is a wedding coming up, a couple of friends, to be specific, Doc and Fr. John, thought they would stop by and throw you a little bachelor party! Fr. John said he has two very well-aged bottles of Irish whiskey that are at their prime and need to be opened. So, being the kind gentleman that he is . . ." Her sentence was interrupted by a big kiss and cheers from all. "To the groom!"

As Frank, Little Joe, and I settled in to watch the game, I thought, *Joe, you are one lucky guy, especially if you count still being alive after everything that has happened and then getting married to a beautiful woman who actually wanted to marry me in high school, which I can never talk about again on pain of death. And then soon to become the father, the actual father of, what else can you call them but Saviors!* I shook my head, shot my whiskey down, and sat back and watched the game as the women, now a bonded threesome, cooked dinner.

Frank and I had another beer and shot combination as we watched the game and waited for dinner to be served. I thought *All I had today was coffee and the last piece of pie from Thanksgiving. Well, a couple of beers or so and a shot, well, maybe a few shots, and I was still, to say the least, starving.*

And just as Mary said, "Dinner is served. Where are those two? But two knocks on the door announced their arrival as they let themselves in. Fr. John carried two exceptional packages designated for after dinner, and Doc had a couple of bottles of wine for dinner. So, they were well received by all.

For the short time it actually took the ladies to put the meal together, it was outstanding. The elk roast had been slow roasting all day, and the scalloped potatoes, made last night with bacon and home-grown onions and potatoes from Red's garden, were piping hot as they came out of the oven. Margie had brought ice cream and a hot fudge topping with just a touch of mint. What a meal!

There was 'almost' no room left for the Irish whiskey, and the word 'almost' didn't even cross the guy's mind. It was going to be flowing as soon as the ladies, now a bonded foursome, cleared off the table and returned to 'the room' for more of their work on the dress.

As Fr. John opened the aged whiskey, the essence of very old, excellent whiskey permeated the room. I got up and brought to the table five brandy snifters and five short glasses of hot water. Fr. John looked at me and said,

"Five, Joseph?"

And I said, "I think a wee one for my namesake, Joseph, would be appropriate for the first toast, wouldn't you think so, Father?"

Fr. John says, "That is if Frank thinks it is okay, and as long as his mother doesn't get wind of it? Right, Little Joe?"

"Yes, sir, I mean, she won't hear it from me," said Little Joe. So, Fr. John poured, and everyone put their snifter on the hot water and slowly rolled it in the glass to warm the whiskey oh so gently. Then, Fr. John offered to make the first toast. "Joseph, if I may?" said Fr. John.

"By all means," I said, "Make it short if you would be so kind. My tongue wants to taste the depth of the age of this whiskey."

"Gentlemen, please raise your glasses to Joseph, a man of great courage, wisdom, and just plain guts. God himself trusts you, and may he guide you on your path forward! To Joseph."

Then all say, "Joseph!"

Little Joe grimaced a little but really didn't let it show as he took his 'sip' like a grown-up.

Little Joe went back to the game, and the men sat, drank out of shot glasses now, told stories, and generally just relaxed and had a good time. Well, I was the happiest I had been in a long time. I really only had a few friends, and these guys were 'them.' Mary knew we would get hungry, so earlier in the day, she and Red made up some dip and chips, as well as a plate of ham, cheese, turkey, pickles, and Red's canned jalapeno slices. Throw in several beers, and the party was a major success!

The ladies came out of the 'room' and looked at the guys as the last of the two bottles of whiskey were emptied: one last shot for Fr. John and one for me. To which I said, "Thanks, guys. This was the last thing I expected, but man, it was worth it. That was some of the best whiskey I have ever had. Thanks, Father!"

Fr. John said, "I think it was a very worthy cause, don't you fellows think so?" A "yes" was said by all, and even Little Joe joined in, which resulted in Frank getting a 'questioning look' from Lucy.

Mary looked at the group and said, "Looks like it was a worthy cause." Doc goes, "I stopped a while ago and ate plenty, not even counting dinner, so I am driving Fr. John home."

Mary said, "But be careful with him. I need him on Wednesday." She smiled and looked as happy as a lark with a bowl full of sunflower seeds, all for herself!

As Doc, Margie, and Fr. John left, Lucy and Frank got their beds ready, and Mary got a sheet and blankets for Little Joe. So that left Red and me to clean up, which really wasn't much of a task at all.

Red said, "You could have at least saved one shot of that whiskey for me."

I smiled and said, "Do you really think I would forget you? But wait a minute for me. I will have a shot of the 'other' stuff with you as you slowly mind you, savor that one."

She took a sip, swirled it on her tongue, and said, "And you didn't save me more than one!" She smiled. That is the best whiskey I have ever tasted!"

Mary walks by and says, "Only about twenty-six days, guys. Twenty-six days!"

And then everyone turned in. Tomorrow was the day before the wedding, and at the moment, the only major issue on the horizon was that it had started snowing, and not just gently. This storm looked like it had blizzard potential. Only time will tell if a change of venue is required for Saturday, which I have not brought up yet.

I headed for my room, and Red was bunking with Mary, which was okay because she had a queen-sized bed. They were both headed to bed as well.

As my head hit the pillow, my last thought was, *Day after tomorrow, I will have a wife in bed with me. And as strange as it seemed, it made me happy to my core.* And then sleep took me.

I woke up early and checked the weather. The snow was coming down as hard as I had seen in a very long time, and it didn't look to be slowing one little bit from what I saw last night. I started a pot of coffee and waited by the fireplace for it to brew.

While I was waiting, Mary got up, and I asked, "Well, do you want the good news or the bad news first?"

Mary looked perplexed, thought for a moment, and said, "Knowing you, they are probably the same, but I will go with the bad news first. What is it?"

I looked at her and said, "You know me better than I thought; they are the same. This storm is bad, and according to the news that I just heard, it looks like the skiers will be ecstatic, but you and I, not so much."

Mary quickly grabbed a cup of coffee and said, "How so?"

"Well," I said, "the meteorologist on Channel 4, and you do know you can't really trust a meteorologist. But he said that this storm shows no movement to the east anytime soon. He went on to say that the Four Corners area will be hardest hit, with two to three feet of snow falling through at least tomorrow afternoon and longer in the mountains, which, as you know, we live in."

"With that said, what do we do about our wedding?" said Mary, fighting back tears as others got up, sat down, and listened to what I was about to say. It was early, but I got up and had a shot and another cup of coffee.

Then I said, "The way I see it, we have two choices. First, and the most unlikely, is that the snow slows down enough to make it to the church before the ten o'clock projected start time of the wedding.

Or, with the aid of four-wheel drives, snowmobiles, and some courageous souls, we have the wedding here." The 'silence' was deafening as Lucy got up and walked around the living room, looking for areas of concern, and really found nothing that couldn't be moved or removed from the room.

Then she said, "Mary, I think we can do it here. I know it sounds crazy, but I have been to weddings in smaller places than this. I mean, look at the chapels in Vegas." And then, Margie said, "We have all the food here, including the cake, and I also have flowers from my greenhouse for the bouquet.

All we would really need would be some chairs, a few candles, some dried flowers, and such, and I really think we could pull it off. We could have the actual ceremony in front of the fireplace; the boys, 'Men, I said,' can enter from Joe's room. Mary, you and the bride's party can come out of the spare room. Pull the couch and chairs to the south wall. We can come up with an aisle between the chairs. There really aren't going to be that many people here anyway, so everything should fit. And by the way, Mary, who is walking you down the aisle?"

Mary blushed through her tears, beamed, and said, "My best friend, Red. I know it's not 'protocol,' but it works for me, and I am the bride and the one who counts!"

Now, it was Red's turn to blush. To cover Red's embarrassment, I said, "I really think it will work, Mary. And it will be something we can tell the children about, over and over until they tell us to stop."

That brought applause from the crowd. I went on, "But we did have to make sure that Fr. John makes it through the storm if we have to call Santa and his sleight to get him here." And as I said, I had a thought. A sleigh ride! That is what I can give her as a wedding gift. It will be perfect, especially *if the snow gives up after the actual wedding.*

And then it started. Everyone pitched in and helped. Frank and I took Frank's four-by-four Bronco and headed to the church for the chairs, candles, and dried flowers. We found some ribbon in a closet and an old cross that had seen its better days but would be perfect behind Fr. John.

Fr. John was there and helped as much as possible. He even found a ring bearer's pillow that had been left behind from a wedding last summer, which Little Joe could walk down the aisle with. To top off everything, he remembered he had a cassette tape with the wedding march and exit music on it for outside ceremonies.

Then he agreed to come back to the house with us to make sure he would be there in case the storm got even worse. He said, "He had slept on many floors during his time in Italy, especially in the small rural area churches where he preached as a young priest." So, with that settled, we were on our way back. We only had to use Frank's wench three times to get out of the snowbanks, but all that ends, well, no matter the problems, is worth it.

Frank and I discussed possible escape plans to Idaho as we were going both to and from the church, so we had that pretty well laid out if all hell broke loose.

Mary, the kids, and the dogs would head up through Colorado, depending on the time of year and the weather. We would stop just North of Ogden, Utah, at a mutual friend of ours. Then, if everything went right and they left at the crack of dawn, they could be at Frank's commune, to use a better word for a survival village, by late afternoon the next day. So, we basically killed two birds with one stone.

We pulled up in front of the house, and with the work of many hands, our living room was transformed into a wedding chapel. Mary cried almost the whole time and thanked everyone until I said, "Mary, sit down and have a glass of wine. We are almost done, and in case you hadn't noticed, you, my soon-to-be wife, are, shall we say, 'pregnant.'" Which got a cheer out of all present, who were finishing up the last touches of ribbon on the chairs, and the 'Wedding Chapel' was complete.

I looked out the window and said, "Looks like we made the right choice. Fr. John, did you tell anyone that the wedding is at my house tomorrow at ten if they can make it, but don't risk it without a snowmobile or at least a four-by-four or a dogsled to get here."

"Yes," said Fr. John. "And might I have a glass of wine? Wedding preparations make me very thirsty." And there were many seconds to that motion. The couch and chairs on the south wall were moved near the fireplace just for the evening so people could sit and drink their wine as a makeshift meal was being prepared. All were very proud of what they accomplished, which I thought they should be. Now, all I have to say is, "I do" tomorrow without fainting, and everything will be just fine as I sipped a shot of the 'good whiskey' I saved for myself from last night. Wise move, Joe, wise move, as I savored another sip.

Everyone hit their beds early because tomorrow would be a long day for all. I sat in a chair next to the fireplace. Mary came over to me and snuggled in. She put her arms around my neck and asked quietly, "Joe, are you really ready for all this? And I don't just mean getting married and all, but really 'All' of this going forward?"

As I sipped the last of the good whiskey and thought for just a few seconds. I said, "Mary, I am ready to be your husband, to be the father of your children as long as I live, and fight the Devil himself if need be just to be at your side. I hope that answers your question?"

Mary, with tears in her eyes, says, "Yes, Joe. That answers my question with an answer I could only expect from a real man like you! I love you with my heart, my mind, and my soul.

Now, all I have to say is 'I do' without passing out, and everything will be right in my world. And you are making it so. Good night, my love. May God and his angels keep you safe." With that, she got up and headed for bed, but not before blowing me a kiss as she went into 'her' room for the last time.

I stoked the fire, threw on one more log, and then positioned the screen to make sure no sparks would fly out. Then, I headed to 'my' room for the last time. I prayed quietly for God to keep all safe and that they all would sleep soundly, even Fr. John, who was quietly snoring on the floor as I passed by.

I woke up about two in the morning as I heard the county snowplow cutting at least one track through the snow in case of emergencies in the area. It's a tough job on a night like this. But that meant there would at least be a track with much less snow, maybe a foot or so, by morning. And then, surprisingly, it was morning.

I woke refreshed to the sounds of people. And if I were going to guess, I would imagine all the ladies were in the kitchen.

I threw on my robe and headed for the coffee pot. All were there except Mary, who had been sleeping later, as the children took more and more of her strength as they came nearer to being born. Lucy handed me a cup of coffee and pointed to a chair by the fireplace. The one next to it held Fr. John with his Bible open, drinking coffee.

Fr. John looked up and said, "I figured that would be you. How did you sleep? I slept like a log. Sleeping on the floor reminded me of my old days in Italy. But I asked how you slept.

I answered, "I slept as if the angels themselves held me in their arms. And that is the truth. I am so glad that today is finally here that you couldn't believe it. And for the wedding to actually be here at the house, really, to me, is the icing on the cake!"

Fr. John looked around the room and quietly said, "I really couldn't agree more." Then we just sat and drank our coffee. Although, I did go get us a touch of a "warm-up of whiskey," just to make it go down just a bit smoother. And Fr. John solemnly said as I poured, "You are a saint amongst sinners, my son." Then we both sat back and relaxed and let the world go on around us. Because for at least this one day, all should be right, at least in this 'little bit of heaven' as it is often called hereabouts.

The time was quickly approaching, and it seemed that all of a sudden, the ladies shifted into high gear. They were in their natural element, and it showed. Every one of them had their job and were flying to get it done. They had set nine as the time for completion of all necessary tasks, and it looked like they would be hitting their targets. The men were, if I were to say, the wedding 'slave labor.' All in all, this really gave us something to do.

Then, when the clock struck nine, we all stood back and admired. What had been a bachelor pad, to some extent, had been transformed into a beautiful wedding chapel. I said with absolute amazement, "The truth be told, I really thought it could be done, but wow! It is gorgeous."

Now came the moment of reckoning. The men adjourned to my bedroom with a bottle of whiskey. The ladies adjourned to the ladies' room du jour with a bottle of champagne. The guests, the ones that made it, and most did due to the snowplow at two in the morning, were all seated. The men filed out at nine fifty, with Fr. John in his wedding robes; I was in my tux, albeit with black cowboy boots, and the others in suits and ties. The candles were lit, and the stage was set.

We all waited patiently until the clock struck ten and the music started. The bridesmaids walked in and took their places. I looked over at Frank and saw him basically beaming as he watched Lucy, his loving wife and matron of honor, take her place opposite of him. Following closely was Little Joe stoically doing his ring bearer job.

He stops first in front of his mother and presents the groom's ring to her. Then, crossing over, he presents the bride's ring to his father, the best man. Then, as the wedding march started, the flower girl, Nancy, had a small basket of rose petals that she threw into the air, much to the amusement of all present, as she walked down the aisle. Then, and I will never forget how beautiful Mary looked with Red at her side as they proceeded forward and reached the front, and Fr. John asked, "Who giveth this woman away?"

Red said, "It is my pleasure to Father." She kissed Mary on the cheek and then took her seat, crying and smiling all the way there. Mary walked up and handed her bouquet to Lucy, who in turn gave her the groom's ring. And on cue, Frank handed me the bride's ring. Then Mary turned to face me with her veil still drawn down.

Fr. John said, "Mary and Joseph, please join hands as I say a few words. To all. It is my pleasure, no, it is the realization of my life's dream to marry these two souls. . . two souls to be joined in matrimony as one soul. . . for in this and only this case, forever in the eyes of God."

Fr. John continued, "I shall begin with Joseph Peter Everlasting. Joseph, do you truly love Mary?"

I looked at her lovingly, gripped her hands firmly, and said, "With all of my heart, mind, and soul."

And then Fr. John turned to Mary and said, "Mareilene Johnson, do you truly love Joseph?"

Mary looked at me lovingly, gripped my hands tightly as I grabbed hers, and said, "With all of my heart, mind, and soul, and the same of my children."

Then, a beaming Fr. John said, "Without further need for anything, I will ask the following question. Joseph, do you take Mary to be your wife, to have and to hold forever?" I answered, "Yes, Mary, forever!"

"Now, Mary," said Fr. John. "Mary, do you take Joseph to be your husband, to have and to hold, forever!"

Mary answered, "Yes, Joseph, forever, until the end of time, I swear to God!"

And then Fr. John said in a soft voice, barely able to be heard, but was, by all gathered there. "Now, Joseph, place Mary's ring on her finger. Well done, and Mary, please do the same for Joseph. Again, well done."

Then, with a big smile on his face and tears of joy in his eyes, Fr. John turned to me and said, "Joseph, you may now kiss the bride." I turned to Mary, lifted her veil, and in her eyes were tears of pure love. I reached over, cradled her chin in my hand, and lifted as my other held the back of her head gently. I bent and kissed her tenderly at first and then with a passion that coursed through me and into her. And she did the same. Although only seconds, they seemed forever, as we parted, and both said "I Do" again. As Fr. John beamed with pleasure, he said, "I now have the highest honor ever bestowed upon me, to pronounce you Joseph and you Mary, husband and wife. May God Himself bless this union, amen! To all gathered here, may I be the first to present to you, Mr. and Mrs. Everlasting!" said Fr. John as tears flowed down his face.

As Mary and I turned to walk back down the aisle, Lucy handed her the bouquet. Those in attendance followed as we proceeded. At the end of the aisle, all the ladies gathered; Mary looked, and then she turned her back and tossed the bouquet into the crowd of ladies.

It was somewhat symbolic since all in attendance were already married, but you wouldn't believe who caught the bouquet. Nancy, the little flower girl, whose mother said, "She could keep it for some time in the distant, very distant future."

Then, to Mary's questioning look, Lucy handed her a warm jacket, a blanket, and a heavy scarf. She looked at me, and I said, "Your carriage awaits, my wife." I donned a warm jacket as well, and we headed out the door to a hail of rice.

And there stood, much to Mary's surprise, a sleigh drawn by none other than Duke and Daisy, their two horses, impatiently waiting for riders so they could warm up.

Mary says, "What, when, and where did you come up with a sleigh?"

"My lady," I said, "This is your wedding present. It was all that I could think of that could even come close to matching this day. So please, Mary, my wife, get in because we need to move before the sleigh freezes to the ground." I took her in my arms and lifted her in, and she wrapped up in the blanket just enough so I could snuggle close to her as I jumped into the other side of the sleigh. We needed just a little push to get moving, but soon, moving we were.

Mary turned to me with love in her eyes, kissed me hard, and said, "Mr. Everlasting, you never cease to amaze me!" And just as we left the cabin, the snow stopped, and the sun shone brightly, as if God just wanted a peek at us. We went up the road for about twenty minutes or so before turning around because the temps were nearing zero, and the horses were saying, 'About time.' As we approached the cabin, I pulled directly into the barn, quickly unhitched the horses, and led them to their stalls. Each stall was ready with a large portion of oats mixed with sugar cubes, which they eagerly dove right into. Mary kissed me again and said, "Thank you so much! I never would have. . ."

She never finished, as I kissed her long and deep and said, "I got you, and that is all I want, well, except these two as well." We walked into the house to cheers of congratulations, and the wedding party was on. Gifts were opened, the cake was eaten, hugs were given, and lots of champagne was enjoyed, not to mention the whiskey and all the food.

After all was said and done, the guests who had to travel home were gone, and the living room was back to semi-normal. It was near nightfall, and everyone was ready to relax, have one more drink before bed, and then, if at all possible, sleep until noon tomorrow. I shared a glass of champagne with Mary and then picked her up, took her into her new bedroom, and closed the door. I had cleared out space for all of Mary's stuff, and she slowly got undressed in front of me for the first time. Then she said, "I am not quite what most husbands expect in their bed the first night, but there will be many others."

And I, naked as well, held her close against me and said, "Tonight, we consummate our love, Mary. We will take care of the other matters later; I promise, my wife, we will."

As we crawled between the sheets and pulled up the blankets, we held each other close and kissed passionately: a kiss of lovers starting a new life of wonder that the world had no idea about.

Then Mary kissed me one more time and said, "Joe, words cannot describe what I am feeling at this moment. And what you mean to me. I promise to make you happy when you are sad, strong when you are discouraged, and to love you and be at your side forever." And all I could say was, "Ditto." Then she kissed me one more time with her eyes sparkling in the moonlight and, with a gentle caress below, whispered in a very sensual low voice, "Soon."

Then she rolled over, and I wrapped around her. She fell asleep in my arms for the first time. I lay there for a few moments more and thought, *God, thank you for Mary and the kids and for making me what I thought I could never be—a man who is loved like no other on earth. And I promise I will do the best I can in her eyes and yours. Good night.*

CHAPTER SEVEN

As I opened my eyes and my mind started working, albeit slowly, I came to the sudden realization that someone else was in my bed. And I smiled as yesterday, my wedding day, or should I say our wedding day, came racing back to me. I snuggled in close to Mary and wrapped my arms around her. As my hand lightly stroked her naked stomach, I was greeted with a kick against my hand. At first, I thought I had done something wrong, when another, only lighter, or better said, minor kick, followed suit. Then I realized that 'the babies' were letting me know that they were there. If possible, I smiled even more significantly, gently tapped twice, and was rewarded with two more resounding kicks. Mary, being used to it, didn't even move at all.

I kissed Mary on the back of her neck and said, "Good morning, Mrs. Everlasting; how did you sleep your first night as a married woman? And the babies told me hi, via foot language."

Mary yawned, and then it dawned on her what I had just said. She rolled toward me and said, "What did you just say?"

I smiled at her and said, "I said, the babies said 'hi' via foot language. They kicked my hand as it lay on your stomach."

She chuckled and said, "They are rather active first thing in the morning, especially when my bladder is full! Which it is, please excuse me."

I admired her as she walked across the room, and of course, she caught me and smiled, "Have you never seen a nine-month pregnant woman before?" as she laughed and disappeared into the bathroom.

"Well, no," I admitted, "but I do think you do look rather beautiful if you ask me."

"Liar."

That was all I heard because the bathroom door closed.

As I got up, I put on pajama bottoms, slippers, and a robe. I looked in Mary's side of the closet and found her bathrobe and slippers. I handed them to her as she came out, and I said, "I think you might need these if you would like a cup of coffee."

She struck her tongue out and headed toward the kitchen, and I asked, "Is that how it is going to be every morning?" I smiled at her as she looked back.

"No, this is," she said as she stepped back into my waiting arms and gave me a long, deep, and loving kiss.

"Now that is more like it!" I said as we held hands and went into the kitchen. Red was up, the coffee was hot and intense, and the sweet rolls melted in my mouth. As I sat there, I thought, *Life is good, and I wish it would always be good. And as much as I hated myself for ruining my mood. I had to wonder about what the 'Prince of Darkness' was up to now. It was now my life, and I knew it and accepted it. I wanted to head it off at the pass, if at all possible.*

If I only knew what was happening in the realm of hell, I probably would be puking my guts out at this moment and would be looking for somewhere safe for 'my' family. But the only place I knew right now that was 'safe' for my family was here.

Here, in the 'Wilds of Colorado,' I am, at this moment in time, God's instrument, put in charge of the very lives of Mary, our children, and all those around us who believe. Some of their beliefs will most certainly be different than mine, and I respect that. But what Doc said, what now seems so long ago, 'You are the one, Joe, you are now the leader. And then he went on to say, 'Whether or not you want to be. I know it is a heavy burden, but I know you are capable of it better than any man alive! Why I feel that way, I don't know, but I know I am right, somehow. I only hope that God will allow me to live up to do what must be done.

But unknown to me, my instincts weren't far from the mark. The Prince had just returned to his realm and was delighted, no, very ecstatic with himself in that he foiled three additional attempts by God to send down a savior to redeem the earth and all who had faith, no matter what their sins were. Be it anything from blasphemy, slave trafficking, murder, rape, and all other capital sins, as long as they still had one iota of hope in their lives of salvation, they were still his, and he intent on saving them from hell!

And if you counted the fiasco in Colorado, he foiled four, albeit two were questionable saviors in less than a year. He thought to himself, *God must be getting more than just a little worried about the state of Earth at this point for him to be sending so many potential saviors to their deaths at his hands.*

At this, he laughed out loud and called for the first of many souls that he would devour this night in celebration of his successes. His minions had done their work well, and he would commend them with the carcasses after he was done with his, let's say, pleasure!

No, he thought, *that wasn't a good enough description. When he was done with the slow and deliberate debauchery of every victim, which would end in his devouring of their very souls, each one of those souls made him stronger and stronger. Still, there was only one problem with the souls of the basically inhuman beings his minions brought to him. Their souls were tainted by 'Him,' so his hunger was never satiated, ever!*

He had only ever had one pure soul, and he would remember it forever. It haunted his nightmares, which he usually enjoyed, but that one soul was why he was cast down from heaven in the first place. And he would never, ever forget that day. It was such a bittersweet memory.

As he sat there and thought to himself, *he was never so happy to get off the surface, but over the last month or so, it was his services that were needed, not his minions. But he had to give them credit since they did get him some souls.* He much needed to rebuild his strength, and since *he was in such a great mood, he would share, just this once.*

When Felix brought Jose and his family to him a couple of days ago, Thanksgiving Day on the surface, what a delicious treat! Jose was saved for last so he could watch his family become soulless living, doing only his bidding for all of eternity!

Then, to show the others his pleasure with Felix's 'gift,' he decided to give Felix Jose for his pleasures; even though Felix didn't yet know it, the 'gift' of Jose tied Felix to the Prince even more than he ever thought. To Felix, he said, "Felix, you did such a good job in that town in Colorado. What is its name?" Felix said, "Master, it is named Cortez."

"Ah yes, Cortez," said the Prince. Felix, as I just said, you did a great job and should be rewarded. As such, that man, Jose, is yours tonight. I know who serves me well! Take him and enjoy him, and make sure the others know why you get him too, just yourself. You do understand what I mean?"

"Yes, My Prince! You can count on that," said Felix.

I shook off the thoughts of Hell and put myself back in a good mood by thinking about the wedding and what could have been a disaster. It turned out better than anyone could have ever imagined. And that put me in not just a good mood but a great one. I knew I had to make another trip into Cortez to check out Jose's and ascertain what Felix was up to. Or if, as he had said, he might leave Cortez and move on. Which definitely wouldn't break my heart, but the trip had to be made. But since the roads were going to be snowed in for at least the next few days after the Wedding Blizzard, I wasn't going anywhere soon. So, I had time to think about better things, like the two cradles I was working on and keeping Mary from wandering out to the barn for eggs or something.

So when I wasn't working on the cradles, they were well hidden behind several bales of alfalfa. But even being nine months pregnant, as a man, women, especially pregnant women, are always unpredictable.

Now, since it was December 2, if everything went according to someone above and his plans, we had about three weeks to kill, getting ready for the births that would shake the world to its core. And I thought, *Hopefully, not quite all the way to the core, Joe. Not that deep. We dodged one bullet, I think, at least for a while. Hopefully, I pray for a while, so help me, God.*

I fed the horses and checked out the sleigh and thought, The weather is excellent to get Mary out of the house and her mind on anything other than just waiting now for the delivery. The fresh air, snow, and another sleigh ride just might fit the bill. I think a winter picnic using the sleigh might be the best thing to get her out of the house to see the crystal-blue skies, with the pinion jays cawing in the trees, and leaving behind the thoughts of giving birth to not only twins but God's twins, if only for a little while! Yes, Joe, you are a genius.

I came into the house and grabbed a cup of coffee. Thankfully, Red had just made a fresh pot, and it tasted delicious. I turned on the TV to the local station, and with a mission in mind, I particularly paid attention to tomorrow's weather. The weather guy was quite a geek, but unlike others, he knew meteorology as well as I did, if not even better. He said, "That tomorrow, unlike the last week, was, in his terms, ideal. Gentle breezes, no clouds, and a nice warm sun to take the cold snap away that the area was under presently and put it to bed, at least for a day or so."

I could have kissed him. I was so happy to hear that great forecast! And to celebrate; I had a hard-earned shot because of the forecast and my plans, not to mention all the work I did in the barn this morning. And even dressed for the weather, it was still damn cold out there. And just as I finished my shot, Red walked in and said, "A little bit early, even for you being out in the cold for quite a while; what's up?"

I blushed because I had been caught in the act, but as I explained my winter picnic via a sleigh ride", she forgave me, but just this time. Red goes on, "So what am I making for this picnic? And I am sure Mary (who was in the shower) isn't supposed to know about it. With that said, when is the picnic?"

"Tomorrow about noon. And I would think, if you can pull it off, some fried chicken, potato salad, pickles, and some of your very 'special' rolls would be great. I will take care of rugs for the dogs, a tarp, and a blanket to lay on top of it. You can throw in a bottle of wine and corkscrew, and I'll take my flask. To be on the safe side from critters, and I do mean the animal type, I will be taking my 9mm just in case. Can you think of anything I have missed?"

Red goes, "I guess we are having fried chicken, potato salad, and, of course, my 'special' rolls for dinner, and the picnic basket will be a piece of cake. And speaking of cake, do you want any dessert? I was planning on making some of my almost famous chocolate chip cookies this afternoon. Would you like a few in the basket, just in case," she said with a smile.

And I said, "Red, did you even know that you are a special lady in my eyes and always will be." "Thanks, you're most welcome, kind sir," said Red with a smile and tears in her eyes. "Now, get out of my kitchen; I have work to do for dinner."

I said, "Just after I have another shot, my 'special' lady." I jumped out of the way of a snapping towel as the shot went down my throat, and I choked on it. "See what you get!" said Red.

At that point, Mary, in her bathrobe, with her hair wrapped in a towel, says, "What's going on out here?"

Red replied, "Joe is a bad boy and just got in a bit of trouble with me.

"Right, Joe."

"Yes," I said, still coughing, and Mary couldn't help noticing the shot glass in my hand and said, "Good job, Red. Keep at least one eye on him at all times; you never know when he might get in 'trouble' again."

They both laughed, but not me. I was still coughing. Mary says, "What are we having for dinner, and what can I help with?" Red goes, "I guess that depends on whether you like skins on your potato salad or not."

"Yes, to skins and what else? I hope you have fried chicken and your 'special' rolls. I heard that part of the conversation as I was drying off. And chocolate chip cookies with double chips, my favorite, hmmm!" "So, Joe, what have you been up to this morning?" said Mary.

"Just the usual: cleaning stalls, feeding cows and horses, you know, all the fun stuff you are going to be doing after your condition improves greatly," I said with a smile.

"Yeah, right!" as if I won't have both hands full of these two, almost all the time, and then some," said Mary.

"So I guess you will be doing those chores for quite a while yet, even after my 'condition' improves greatly. Right, Red?"

"Well, to tell the truth, I haven't ever been pregnant, so I have an idea, but nothing hands-on. My husband, God rest his soul, couldn't have children, but my sisters did, and I babysat a lot. With that said, I know kids, but not that way."

Mary says, "I'm sorry, Red, I didn't mean to bring up bad memories."

"You didn't believe me. I lived a life with a husband that I loved and who loved me, and I was pleased. And then God led me to Joe and then to you and the babies as well. How blessed can one woman be," she said through tears, not of pain, but of joy, as she hugged us both.

Now, back to those special rolls. We all laughed and pitched in, and quickly, everything was getting ready for dinner. The eggs and the potatoes were boiling on the stove, the chocolate chip cookies with double chocolate chips were baking in the oven, and the special rolls were rising on the counter. With all that going well, we sat down and discussed the next twenty or so days of December and what yet needed to be done.

The afternoon was lazy, and we all went for a slow walk to work up an appetite for dinner and ran into Doc and Margie, who were snowbound as well and were eager to get out of the house. Doc said they were coming over to check up on Mary, who was really in good spirits and feeling not great, but for nine months or so pregnant, not bad at all, and thought it would be a great excuse to visit the neighbors and hoped Red just might be making something, delicious.

Then Mary told them about our simple dinner of fried chicken, potato salad, and Red's special rolls, and of course, Margie said they didn't want to intrude!

Doc found Mary fit as a fiddle, and he and Margie were both pleased. They stayed for dinner, which they tried to say they couldn't, but the smell of the fried chicken was too much, and they were hooked as dinner companions for the evening. All in all, this was a good thing because Mary's mind was off the pregnancy and enjoying the company.

Doc pulled me to the side before the dinner was served and said, "I have been told that wolves had been spotted up the valley early this morning due to the blizzard, and Richard had lost a heifer to a pack just before daylight. So, if I planned anything outside, I better just be prepared."

Thinking about the picnic planned for noon, I moved it up to eleven, and it would be moved even closer to the house just in case. I would be carrying two 9mm's with extra magazines. When Red was alone, I told her I had moved up the time, and of course, I had to tell her why.

I said, I don't expect any trouble, but I will have the two dogs, which are part wolf themselves. Two 9mm's, just in case. I told her that Mary knew how to shoot well. So we would be okay, and Red relented, and she said, "Just make it a quick picnic, promise?"

And smiling at her, I said, "Yes, Mother," and got punched in the shoulder, just for good measure. Red headed for the table like there was nothing in the world to worry about. The meal was a great success; Doc and Margie said their goodbyes. Everyone was exhausted, and good nights were said.

Waking up early and looking out the window, the day dawned bright and clear without a breath of wind. I went out on the pretense of feeding the horses, which I actually did, and then after they were done, I treated each of them, Duke and Daisy, to some sugar cubes, and they looked at me, like, what did we do to deserve these? But of course, they didn't turn me down, as they munched them down noisily.

Then, out came the sleigh harness, and they knew they had been duped, but to get out would be great. And there were almost always oats and more sugar cubes after their morning outing.

I could almost read their minds as I harnessed them up. And I was smiling and looking forward to the 'jaunt' as much as they were. As I entered the house, Mary was watching Red scurrying around the kitchen and knew something was up. But Red wasn't talking, and I was her next strategic target. She cornered me at the door and said, "Okay, mister, what's up? And me, trying to play dumb, which didn't work, finally relented and said, "Well, sweet love of mine, we are going on a picnic in the sleigh, so go get your warm coat and boots, and be back out here in five."

She smiled and hurried toward the bedroom while I headed for the kitchen. Red said, "You remember our talk from last night, right?"

"Yes," I said, turning to show her my two loaded 9 mm and pulling out the extra magazines in my jacket pocket.

"Okay, be careful because if you get killed, I'll kill you! Well, you know what I mean," said Red.

"Yes, I do, and I am trained better than anyone you know with these babies (pointing to my 9mms) or anyone you have ever known or will know, with the possible exception of Frank. He is the only one who might be better, and I mean might, okay?"

Red just shook her head, said yes, handed me the basket, and said, "Be safe." Then she went and poured a shot and a cup of coffee, walked by me with both of them and sat down in front of the fire to wait for our safe return.

Mary came out of the bedroom, all bundled up, and we headed to the barn with her arm in mine, happy as a clam. I helped her into the sleigh, and away we went.

We headed to the south, about a mile or so, to a lovely little meadow *with a line of boulders to our backs to be on the safe side,* I thought. We pulled up, and I turned the horses toward home and got out the tarp, blanket, and dog rugs as Mary grabbed the basket.

Within a few minutes, we were munching on cold fried chicken, potato salad, and Red's special rolls. The dogs waited somewhat patiently for tidbits. The flask came out, and a glass of wine for Mary was poured, and the day really couldn't have been more perfect and downright beautiful.

As Mary cleaned up and put everything back in the basket, I suddenly knew something was wrong, very wrong!

I heard voices in my mind. They were crude and almost incoherent, and for some reason, God only knows, I could listen to wolves thinking and approaching very fast.

"Mary!" I yelled. "Take this 9mm and cock it. Don't argue; do it NOW! We have a terrible problem approaching fast from the north. Be ready to shoot as needed, don't argue, just do it, NOW!"

Mary moved as fast as possible and was in the sleigh with the gun cocked and ready. I said to Mary, "I can hear rapidly approaching wolves 'talking' with the lead saying we are only seven, but they have no idea we are here."

And then they were right on top of us as the leading two wolves headed straight for the horses. But Duke and Daisy, raised in the mountains, knew what to do to stay alive against wolves. Duke, with a bared mouth full of teeth, grabbed one and Daisy the other. They grabbed them by the neck and audibly snapped each of their necks. Then, their hooves did the rest of the work, and they were dead.

I thought, two down and five to go. Each of the dogs had a wolf to handle and were doing a damn good job. As one of the more aggressive wolves leaped at Mary, she calmly fired a perfect shot to its head from the 9mm, and she held ready for any other.

I took the sixth one not as cleanly, but the second shot finished it off, but not before he 'told' the seventh to get help, and I still had no idea how I could hear their thoughts. But as the seventh turned to go at breakneck speed, I took a calming breath, as this shot would mean life or death for us.

The lone seventh wolf was already over a hundred yards away. I bore down on him with my 9mm and waited just a second for the 'seventh' to jump the drift ahead of him, which by now was about one hundred and twenty-five yards out.

I timed the jump and fired; as number seven went up, the bullet caught him right between the ears before he could say anything. I knew no message had been sent because I had listened for the complete time, which seemed like minutes but had been, in actuality, a matter of seconds.

I was in the sleigh and had it at top speed within a minute, if that long, as the dogs ran beside the sleigh, protecting Mary and the children, each covered in blood from their kills. And to Mary and me, the ranch seemed like it was still miles away!

But then, when I heard the howling of the other pack of wolves coming up fast behind us. I thought we were dead; there it was, the barn, with the doors open, and then we were inside as. I leaped from the sleigh and attempted to close the doors as the wolves hit it, almost pushing them open.

But I yelled, "Not on my watch," as I pushed to close the barn doors with every ounce of strength I had, and then some; the doors inched closer as I could feel and smell their foul breath only inches from my face.

And then, with one last desperate shove, the doors closed, and the drop bar dropped to secure the closure. I knew we were now safe because all the other entrances were closed and locked because of the weather. Had it been summer, the result would have been different, very different!

But I could still hear the wolves outside, talking, thinking, or whatever the hell you wanted to call it, that there was food back at the fighting ground to eat (meaning the dead wolves). Then, their leader thought that after they ate their fill, they would head back up the valley. It was just a little too rough down here! And to think, we thought it was going to be an easy kill.

I relaxed at the good news I'd heard.' At the same time, Mary looked at me and saw me visibly relaxed. She somehow, for some unknown reason, knew that I could actually 'hear them talk.'

And all she said was, "You knew they were coming, and since they were almost silent on the snow, I knew that your 'regular' hearing didn't hear them at all. I don't have a clue how, but you can hear their thoughts, can't you?"

I just crossed myself because I could still hear them outside and knew that they had decided to go back to the fighting ground to basically 'feast' on their brothers. And I said,

"Thank you, God!" I quickly unharnessed the horses and gave them a well-deserved treat. That is when I knew the coast was clear to make it to the house." And that is when I said to Mary,

"Yes, I could hear them, and I could hear them all the way to the house. And I also know that they all have left to go feed on their dead brothers." And since I knew they were all gone to the 'killing ground' to feast on their dead brothers, we quickly went into the house. Mary held on to me for dear life, looking in every direction possible until we were in the house, and the door was locked and double-checked to make sure.

We shed our winter gear, checked out the dogs, and bandaged what needed bandaging, which wasn't much. Being part wolf themselves, their instincts just kicked in, and they fought to the death. And in the course of taking care of the dogs, Red waited impatiently to know what the hell had just happened! And she wanted every single detail. Well, with the exception of me understanding wolf, for some reason, only God knew. She got the complete story from when we left until we ran in and locked the door.

And later that evening, I thought, *God, I don't understand how you let me hear the wolves coming, but without that, we would have been dead. And I just wanted to say thanks yet again!"*

Then, to Mary and Red, I said, "It was not a bad picnic, all and all if I do say so myself."

As the pillows flew, I went on, "I can't wait to tell Frank about that shot on the seventh as he leaped to clear that snow drift. It had to be at least 125 yards. That was a shot for the history books!"

Red rolled her eyes and said, "Soon it will be 150 yards," as she handed me a shot, which I gladly accepted!

Even though Mary had half a glass of wine at the picnic, before being so rudely interrupted," she said to Red, "Might I have a glass of wine, and please, make it a rather big one, if you would be so kind."

Red said, "If you weren't giving birth in a few weeks, I'd give you a whole bottle, especially after making it through that ordeal."

Red thought, *So a larger glass of wine will have to suffice to settle what must be buried fear, which had to be running wild in her right now, but being who she is, she didn't show it. Well, maybe just a tiny bit.*

I got up and looked out the window. Mary noticed but didn't say anything; she just watched for any sign of concern, but there was nothing. So she relaxed, as much as anyone could have after having gone through Hell! I thought, *No sign of anything moving, or more importantly, anything within hearing distance. So I decided now was the time to break the news of the day after tomorrow's trip into Cortez. Which I knew wouldn't go well, but it had to be done just to make sure all was calm and peaceful in their 'Little piece of heaven.'*

Then, I jumped right in with both feet, and I asked. "Well, ladies, which news do you want first? The good or the bad news?"

"About what?" asked Mary.

"That wasn't the question that I asked, as you well know." I said, "The good or the bad news, first? The choice is yours?"

Mary and Red looked at each other and said, together, "The bad, what is it?" Mary asked, rather timidly, after today's 'adventure.'

"Are you sure?" I asked. And they both just shook their heads yes. "Okay, here goes. I know we are running low on essentials, and . . ."

"You're not going into town, are you, Joe?" Mary asked. "And, before I was so rudely interrupted, and liquor, not to mention stopping by Jose's to check the lay of the land so I/we will know where we stand."

The looks on their faces could have killed an ordinary man or at least really injured him beyond belief. "So, mister smart guy," says Red, "What is the good news?"

"Well," I said, "since the snowplow just plowed to the highway this morning, I figured I would wait until the day after tomorrow to go, that is if Red thinks we can get by on what we have in-house for another day."

"We can and will, no matter what," said Red. Okay, the day after tomorrow it is. Mary snidely asks, "Do we really have a choice in the matter?"

I go, "Not really. If Felix is still there, we make one plan, and if he is long gone, we have the liberty to take our time with our long-term planning."

Mary sighed deeply and said, "I guess it makes sense, and we need essentials. And by waiting until the day after tomorrow, the road will be more well-traveled as everybody is in the same predicament as us after the blizzard. The plan is sound, well, as sound as going into a bear's cave in the spring is sound. But as you always say, 'it is always best to know where and what your enemy is and doing, and not to be guessing,' right?"

"Right, you are, my beautiful and brave wife." And as I say it, I mean it more than she will ever know. Red, I will need a list of supplies to last about one week. That should be about right, I would think.

"I will start on it tomorrow if you don't happen to have any more 'news,' or do you?" asked Red.

"No," I said. "But I do have one more 'good' thing after all. I still have a bottle of whiskey, just in case we are running low. And no, Mary, it isn't the good bottle that the Father gave me. That bottle has been stashed away until the babies are born, and I am sure it will be opened 'right after' that." I said to Mary, who gave me a look as you had better save it, mister husband of mine.

CHAPTER EIGHT

The next day, everything returned to normal, well, as normal as it can be, with a blizzard to clean up after, a nine-month pregnant wife, and a very problematic Red fusing and fretting around.

Then, to make it up to both of them, I brought in the cradles, which I had carefully dried slowly in front of a slow-burning hearth in the barn. Mary cried like a baby. I thought, *I hope tomorrow goes as well, and for some reason, I felt at ease about the trip. I trusted that 'feeling' and enjoyed the congratulations on a job well done.*

Tomorrow came too soon for the ladies, so I called Margie and asked her if she would like the company of a couple of snow-bound women while I went into town to survey the situation. And I also wondered if there was anything they needed from town while I was there?"

She said, "I am bored, silly, so that I would enjoy the company. I will have a short list for you when you drop them off." I said, "Works for me," so we all loaded up and headed to Margie's.

I picked up the list from Margie and continued north, but something said go south! Okay, after my talk with God, trusting my instincts, I made a U-turn and headed toward the main road. As I was going south, I heard a voice again near our picnic area. Although very much weaker, it seemed to come from just one lone wolf. As I slowed, the voice in my head said, *please help me*!

Knowing it could be a trap, I slowly stopped and checked the area out from inside my truck. It was a mass of destruction, with bits and pieces of dead wolves everywhere. Obviously, the others did come back to 'feed.' Then, over to the side was one living wolf. I could tell he was still just breathing, but the question was, why was 'he' still alive?

With the coast appearing clear, I grabbed my 9mm, got out, and headed for the lone, living wolf. Again, in my mind, I heard, *Please help me*, only more robust, because he was closer, much closer, and I could see that the wolf was ancient and would die soon.

As I walked toward the wolf, I saw my flask on the ground and picked it up. It had a full bite mark punched in it, and I hoped that it really pissed off the wolf that did it just before he died. I stuck it in my jacket pocket, for the hell of it, and knelt by the wolf, who I knew posed no danger to me.

Strange as it sounds, the rest of the conversation was all in my mind. *'Thank you, human! My kind, especially Black Moon, the leader of the second pack that followed you to your home, or in my language, your den. He thought it fitting that what had been their 'Wolf King' should die slowly whimpering like a puppy until some other beast killed him, or he just plain died.'*

I felt pain, and my heart sickened for an animal that I had feared all of my life as I walked the trails alone, searching out game to kill and eat. A timber wolf! The question in my mind was, what to do? The wolf answered with a simple request! 'Please just cut my throat and let me die with honor.'

As I continued thinking, I knew the wolf was following my every thought. . . 'If I kill you, it will be a knife to your heart! As compensation for your quick death, I have conditions that you will have to consider first.

The wolf thought, 'Okay, that will be an honorable death. What is your condition?'

My condition is as follows, and please listen to it all before you stop me. Deal?

Yes, it's a deal, but first, you need to know a couple of things.

Okay, I listen and learn, and the deal is done. I understand. Go on, for your time is growing short.

The wolf took a ragged breath and continued, 'My name is Death Walker, and for some reason, I have been king of the wolves for centuries.

That is until just recently when I started to age rapidly. I knew my time had come, and now, I understand why. I am supposed to help you with your obligation to God, the maker of all things, including timber wolves.

Now, hear my secret, which I have kept for over a century. There will come a time of dire need for you and your charges, which were given to you by God himself. It will be a time of a battle that will decide who will win this planet: Good or Evil.

At that time, and you will know when it is! All you have to do is yell out to the open sky above you and say, ' The time, Death Walker, is here for you to pay your debt to me. Help me now, I ask in the name of 'God' himself.' At that point, you will see me leading a charge of wolves of all kinds, alive and dead, even congealed dust and bones of wolves. Millions, upon millions, upon millions, will come because of my command to fight alongside you and yours against the evil you face. They will come as I call because I am the king of all wolves; I am 'Death Walker'!

I can't say we will win, but I guarantee we will definitely make it one 'Hell of a fight.' A fight that can make the type of man that I know in my heart that you are the 'Winner' and the 'World,' standing and fighting with you win as well.

The 'Prince of Darkness,' the 'Loser, ' although sadly he cannot really be killed, his power can be highly diminished. He will be banished from Earth long enough for God to save his people and all creatures that believe, and that is enough for me!

I think to Death Walker, now my conditions. After I kill you, I will take your hide and have a taxidermist clean, cure, and oil your fur until it shines. Since eyes do not withstand that process, I will have him search out two made of glass that are coal black, except for specks of white to remind me of stars to be put in place of yours as you take your place amongst the stars above.

And finally, you will hang in my home in a place of honor; I swear it on Mary, mother of Christian and Hope, the coming salvation of the earth. What's left of your body, I will burn in effigy. That is my condition, agreed?

Death Walker thinks to me, 'Joseph Peter Everlasting, God picked a good and wise man in his choice of you. Agreed!

My knife plunged deep and quickly, as Death Walker's last thought, *'I, and all my brothers and sisters, will be there when needed.'* And he died.

I quickly skinned him and then built a small pyre, lit it, and said a prayer of thanks to God! I waited until the fire completely consumed Death Walker. Then I stood, crossed myself, and left. I would never return here again if I could help it. It would just be too painful. I knew I would have to let Mary and Red know. It would be challenging, but once they knew the complete story, they would understand. . . that I knew without any doubt.

After that, and many tears shed, I was in Cortez in about a half hour. I stopped at the east edge of town, dropped off the wolf pelt, and explained in detail what I wanted done. Alexander looked at me with a questioning look but, seeing my determination, said, "It will be done as you requested, to the letter. I will give you a call when it is finished."

Then, as I started to park in front of Jose's, on the door was a sign that read, "For sale. See the Bank of Cortez for details." Well, I thought, so much for Felix. I stopped by my builder's office to get the skinny, and as I figured, he knew a lot. More than a lot. Working with all the contractors he works with, he knew more than I really wanted to know.

According to one of his contractors who saw Jose's work van leaving town late Wednesday night, just before Thanksgiving, and hadn't been seen since. Their burned-out car had been found near Cuba, New Mexico, on Thanksgiving day without sign of any foul play. But also, no bodies of him, his wife, or their two little girls were found. The builder said, "The police had finally given up searching, figuring that they had run afoul after their car broke down and caught fire. They figured that they tried hitchhiking, and . . . Oh, and one other thing. He had seen Felix the day after Thanksgiving." He said, "He was heading north out of town and hadn't been seen since. He reported it to the sheriff, but nothing ever came of it."

I said, "Thanks," and headed to the grocery and liquor stores. Then, I headed east on the main highway. The traffic was light, and after what seemed like only minutes, I took the left-hand turn onto the dirt road to my ranch.

I continued by the house and picked up Red and Mary. I filled them in on what I had learned during my excursion into Cortez. I told them about Jose's Diner being closed and that it was up for sale. According to my builder friend, Jose and his family were missing, and their burnt-out car was found near Cuba, New Mexico.

Sadly, I surmised that Jose and family, being so close to Felix, probably knew more than needed or, for some other reason, were, more than likely, no longer of this world as I thought to myself, as I was sure Red and Mary were as well, *What world. . . Were they part of now?"* The ride back to the house was a quiet one.

Once we were home, all the supplies were unloaded, horses and dogs fed, and we all settled down in front of the fireplace: Mary and me on the couch, Red in the comfy chair by the side of the fire. I decided it was time to bring Red in on the 'Talking to Wolves' thing.

I had told Mary earlier in the day that I was going to tell Red the 'picnic' story and that there was also more that she and Red needed to know about today. Mary's eyes got large, and she asked, "Just what else happened?" I said, "I will tell it all at one time. Does that work for you?" Mary hesitantly said, "Yes."

I got up from the couch and grabbed a glass of wine for Mary and shots for myself and Red, and then I started. "Mary, the first part of what I have to tell you will have you on edge, but the second, well, you will know when you hear it all."

Mary hesitantly says, "Okay, Joe. I trust you, but do your best not to scare me to death, promise?"

"I will do my best, my love," I said as I started my story.

"Red," I said, "Mary and I left something out of our picnic story, and after what happened to me this morning after dropping you guys off, I figured it was time to tell you, Red, the complete 'picnic' story. And to tell you both, as Paul Harvey would say, 'And now, the rest of the story.'

"Red, to be very blunt. The reason that we survived the wolf attack at the picnic wasn't pure luck, as we alluded to when we told the story earlier." At this point, I took a big sip of my shot and continued,

"It was because I heard the wolves coming. Not their noise, but their actual thoughts."

As I let that sink in, I finished my shot, and Red downed hers all in one gulp as she looked at Mary for confirmation. Mary just shook her head yes and had a big sip of her wine as well. Red goes, "Well, I have heard some wild stuff in my time, but this, this really takes the cake. I am getting another Joe. You look like you could use one as well."

I said, "Yes, please, and go ahead and bring the bottle. With what else I have to tell you guys about today, two will not do. Mary can have one more during the telling of this morning's events, but no more. Her bottle stays in the cabinet. I am sure that after the second half of my story, she will need another, but not for any reason that you could imagine, I guarantee."

As I thought to myself, *Tell the picnic story short enough for Mary not to go through the horror of it again but long enough for Red to get the gist of the whole event.* Then I said, "We were just basically finishing up when, for some reason, I heard 'things' in my head, and in a flash, I realized I was hearing the thoughts of wolves coming our way to attack and kill.

Within seconds, I had Mary in the sleigh with my second 9mm cocked and ready, and then they were there. The lead two wolves went straight for the horses, which fought valiantly, having fought wolves several times in their lives in the mountains. Two others went after the dogs, thinking, which I heard, that they should be easy prey, but being half wolves themselves and, more importantly, protectors of the babies and Mary, ripped into the wild ones like they were death itself a coming. Which left Mary, who took out one with a shot between the eyes, as we told you, and I hit the other one, but not killing him.

But what was left out of our telling was I heard that he was telling the seventh wolf to get help just as I shot and killed him. That is how I knew number seven wasn't running away; he was running for help, which would have spelled our doom within minutes. That was how I knew that I had to kill him, and it took all my skill to do just that.

In Mary's defense, she didn't know anything about any of this until we were safe in the barn. That is when she calmed down somewhat and had time to think. Then she put two and two together and spoke.

'You knew they were coming, and since they were almost silent on the snow, I knew that your 'regular' hearing didn't hear them at all. I don't have a clue how, but you could hear their thoughts, couldn't you?'

Then, I just crossed myself because I could still hear them outside, and they had decided to go back to the fighting ground to feast on their dead brothers. That is when I knew the coast was clear to make it to the house." And that is when, to Mary, I said, "Yes, I could hear them, and I could hear them all the way to the house. And I also know now that they all have left to go feed on their dead brothers."

All Red could say was, "Oh my God, Mary, did he leave anything out?"

"No," said Mary. It was even worse than that, but he spared my feelings the best he could. But it was still hell hearing it again. I hope what I haven't heard is better if that is possible. And Red, while you are up getting you know what, just a touch more for me would be greatly appreciated."

Red said, "Of course, to both requests. The spoken and unspoken." Once everyone was served, and in Mary's case, tucked in tighter in her blanket, I continued.

"As you two know, when I dropped you off this morning, I was going north, but I had a feeling that I was going in the wrong direction. So, following my instincts, I made a U-turn and headed south. And since I was heading south, I figured I might as well stop at the picnic site to check and see if we left anything important.

But as I got close, and Mary, please relax. Well, as much as you can, I heard a voice again near our picnic area, although very much weaker, and it seemed to come from just one lone wolf. As I slowed, the voice in my head said, 'Please help me!'

Knowing it could be a trap, I slowly stopped and checked the area out from inside my truck. It was a mass of destruction, with bits and pieces of dead wolves everywhere. Obviously, the others did come back to 'feed.' But over to the side was one intact wolf, and I could tell he was still just barely breathing. The question I had was, why? Why didn't they eat him as well?

With the coast appearing clear, I grabbed my 9mm and headed for the lone, living wolf. Again, in my mind, I heard, *'Please help me.'*

His thoughts were more robust now because he was closer, and I could see that the wolf was ancient and would die soon. I knelt by the wolf, who I knew posed no danger, and in my mind, just like during the 'picnic' wolf attack, I heard the following conversation as if it had been spoken out loud.

Thank you, human! My kind thought was that it was fitting that what had been their Wolf King for centuries and centuries should die slowly, whimpering like a pup.

I couldn't believe it, but I felt heartsick for an animal I had feared all my life. . . a timber wolf! Then, the wolf answered the question in my mind about what to do. *Please just cut my throat and let me die with honor.* At this point, I knew the wolf was following my every thought.

Ladies, I'll make this short and sweet. I consented to kill the wolf with honor if he agreed to my conditions, which he did, but only after I heard him out, to which I decided to, and I told him, '*Okay, I listen and learn. Go on; your time is growing short.*

The wolf thought to me. *My name is 'Death Walker,' and for some reason, I have been King of the Wolves for centuries upon centuries. That was until just recently, when I started to age rapidly. I know my time has come, and now I know why. How I know came to me last night in a dream as I lay here dying.*

I am supposed to help you with your obligation to God, the maker of all things, including timber wolves. Now, hear my secret. And Ladies, this is the important stuff.

Death Walker continued. *There will come a time of dire need for you and your charges given to you by God. A time of a battle that will decide who will win this planet, Good or Evil? At that time, and you will know when it is, look up to the open skies above you and yell, 'The time has come, Death Walker, for you to pay your debt to me. Help me now, I ask in the name of God.'*

At that point, you will see me leading a charge of wolves of all kinds, alive and dead, even congealed dust and bones of wolves who died eons ago. Millions, upon millions, will come because of my command to fight alongside you and yours against the evil you face. They will come as I call because I am the King of all Wolves, I am 'Death Walker'! I can't say we will win, but we will definitely make it one 'Hell of a fight.'

Almost finished, ladies; hang in there. *Now, my condition. Before I kill you, know now that I will take your hide and have a taxidermist clean, cure, and oil your fur until it shines, and you will hang in my home in a place of honor. What is left of your body, I will burn in effigy.*

Death Walker thinks to me, Joseph Peter Everlasting, God picked a good and wise man in his choice of you. Agreed! The knife plunged deep and quickly, and Death Walker's last thought was, *'All my brothers and sisters and I will be there when needed.'*

And then he was gone. I quickly skinned him, built a small funeral pyre, and lit it, and I said a prayer of thanks to God! I waited until the flames consumed Death Walker. I also knew that I would have to tell you guys the story of Death Walker. I knew it would be difficult for you to hear. But I also knew that only you two would really understand and agree with me."

"Mary, after what I just told you, do you have any objection to hanging the pelt in our home?" I asked.

Mary, with tears in her eyes, said, "No, actually, I would be honored. And the story, just as you told it, will be in the journal by tomorrow, this I swear."

Red says, "It should be in there by all means!" Then she looks at me and says, "You continue to amaze me. Now you can talk to wolves. What next? God himself. Oh, wait, you already did that. Joe, you are just the man that Death Walker said you are, and that's all I can actually say to be truthful."

"Red speechless, now that's a first," I said. "Will wonders never cease? Well, I guess around here, probably not."

I grabbed the bottle, poured us another round, and thought to myself, *I am so glad that is done.*

"So, anyone up for a short trip to Durango for a steak dinner? I am starving since you two have decided that I have to lose weight and to do it by not feeding me," I said. And at the same time, I found out it is impossible to dodge two pillows at once. And the steak at Delmonico's was perfect.

CHAPTER NINE

Well, for the first day in a while, we all just sort of slept in. I guess after all the stress and then the great steak. The Colorado Highway Patrol DUI stops along the highway, especially on Friday and Saturday nights, were a regular event. Therefore, we behaved ourselves until we were home.

And then we 'relaxed'. Yes, relaxed was an excellent word for a glass of wine for the pregnant one and beer and shots for the bad kids of the group. But as we were sitting by the fire relaxing, I got a great idea of how to fill up the next few weeks or so with a project for all. I thought to myself, '*wind spinners*' and planned out our morning of going to all the neighbors and getting anything and everything that they wanted to get rid of, that could even catch a breath of wind. I can't wait until tomorrow, Saturday, to head out.

Everyone was just about asleep as I told them my plan for tomorrow morning, and they thought I was crazy. But I said, "Well, okay, you two come up with something better. We would only be in the immediate area, so no worries there. And we would probably be back by noon, or maybe later, but who really cared? What else did we have to do?"

Mary looked deep in thought as she said to Red and me, "Let's do it. We will learn something and, more importantly, kill time. God truly knows I need to kill some time. Because if I don't, I am going to kill something or someone very soon. And last but not least, it will get us out of the house."

Red says, "Yes, I think it is a great idea, but look who thought it up? Maybe we should consider it a little longer," she smiles.

Then morning was upon us, and instead of sleeping in, we were up, not early, but not late either. After a great pot of coffee, no shots in my cup, we had a light breakfast of eggs and bacon, and then we all bundled up and headed out.

Our first stop of the day was Fr. John's house. We knew he was always an early riser and had a barn full of stuff that he just knew he would have a use for someday. As we entered his treasure trove of a barn, we just stopped and stared, and even before we actually started looking, Fr. John said, "You can only search, find, and remove on one condition." And knowing Fr. John as I did, I slowly asked, "And what might that condition be?" Fr. John, without missing a beat, said, "That you, Joseph, have to make me a special wind spinner with articles that you find in here."

"Deal," I said as we went on a mission of discovery. I found what I needed most almost immediately, and why he had them, I don't even think he knew. I found a stack of bicycle wheels: one of the keys to the whole project. I think I came up with about forty or so. At that point, as I told the girls and the Father, really anything that could catch the wind, and that we could find at a minimum of three of, and no maximum really, we got to take.

Then I heard, "I'll be damned, and then a quick, 'Sorry God,' and I knew the Father found just what he needed for his spinner. He had found a box of communion chalices of every shape and size in a box just collecting dust. He got down on his knees and said, "Thank you, Jesus, these will be perfect for my spinner." Then, within minutes, the box of chalices was in the truck with Fr. John smiling to beat all.

Then, as I looked around one final time, I found a box of wooden wheels about ten inches in diameter. They were like what you would have seen on an old-fashioned wheelbarrow. And I could use them with the chalices. I wasn't sure how I was going to use them, but I couldn't pass them up. In the truck, they went, with my name on the box.

Then Fr. John said, "This, my friends, calls for a shot of the 'excellent' stuff. That is except you, Mary. You, my extraordinary friend, get just a little sip of wine for the time being." And I said, "Father, you have been holding out on us," as I smiled and hugged him.

"Well, we all have our secret 'good stuff,' am I right."

Red smiled and said, "Yes, Father, we all do."

Then, after the 'excellent' stuff shots and a touch of wine for Mary, we headed over to Doc and Margie's house, where Mary came across a box of wooden shoes from Holland. Margie looked at the shoes and said, "Take them and see what you can do with them. We have already moved them more than a couple of times, and it is time to use them or lose them. As for a wind spinner made out of them, it's excellent. My garden can definitely use one to at least distract the birds from my veggies.

Then we got busy as we headed out to the next neighbor and the next. At each neighbor's house, we came up with something or things that were unique. And you would not believe what we came up with at our last stop: a box full of coconut shell halves. Mary counted at least twenty or more, which the neighbor had because, being an ex-drama teacher from Cortez High School, the shells were from a performance of South Pacific.

I couldn't believe it and all the other stuff we acquired. We not only had enough for Red's five, but we had enough for the obligations for five more, counting the Father's special one, which I promised I would make if I could find the other parts I needed. If everything worked out, he wouldn't believe his spinner when he received it for Christmas.

Then, returning to the barn, Red and Mary went to the house to grab a snack and facilities. I went to the barn and started a fire first thing to take the chill off. Then, when Red and Mary, with the dogs right beside them, the work really began.

We separated all the 'stuff' into spinner groupings, with many changes as the day went on. The goal was to make a statement about what the designer meant to say/tell the observer. And really, that was the most challenging part. Because we all are strong-willed, to say the least, compromises had to be made. But in the long run, I speak for the group. I think, no, I know, the spinners will be outstanding.

We will have to go into town the day after tomorrow to get a few necessary parts, bearings, and such. But overall, I had the majority of what we needed from all the construction projects I had worked on. And I guess I can say that even if I didn't know what I might use something for, it did come home with me. And now, a lot of it will be put to use after all.

And one other thing. We all decided to go into town. Mary, on the safe side, would be disguised and stay in the truck, but a ride and to get out of the house was just what the doctor ordered. And speaking of which, Doc and Margie would be over in a week, the fifteenth to be exact, for Mary's checkup and dinner and to check on the progress of their one-of-a-kind spinner.

Then, over a light breakfast of coffee, coffee cake (freshly baked by Red this morning), and some cold ham and Red's special rolls, which they now had come to be known as. While we ate, we discussed any distinct 'things', for the lack of a better word they thought would accent their spinners. We figured out where we planned on stopping, and we probably could accommodate their whims and fancies. If not, we would either do without or if we saw a store that might have what Mary and Red were looking for. We would stop and see. You never know.

Everyone was excited about the trip into town. I had two stops in mind for my own needs: the hardware store and the Shining Star antique store. The antique store was a gamble, but I think it could be worth the stop. Since I hadn't ever been in the store, Red and I decided that it was one stop that Mary if she kept a low profile, could come in accompanied by Red. The ladies had a cover story, if needed, of a local neighbor who had just moved into our area.

Mary was so excited that she said, "I just can't wait to get out of this valley, even if it is so beautiful, and to get to see Cortez for the first time in several years." Then I said in response, "It has changed, but most of the changes were more for the tourists."

Red, Mary, and I quickly got dressed, jumped into the truck, and headed into town, leaving the dogs to take care of the ranch house. And we were off to Cortez, like in the Christmas poem, " The Night Before Christmas." 'We flew away like the down of a thistle.'

If the smile of glee on her face was any indication, Mary was like a little kid on an adventure of a lifetime. Even Red seemed excited to be going because since our ordeal started, she had been basically in the house except for a trip to church, going to see Margie and some of the other neighbors, and helping in the barn.

We pulled into town, and the first stop was the hardware store for paint (bright colors), nuts and bolts, welding rods, bearings, spar varnish to handle the weather, and assorted other things I knew we would need but wouldn't know it until I saw them on a shelf or in a box.

That stop went relatively fast overall, considering all we bought. The clerk looked at the strange assortment, and all I said was, "Building Christmas gifts," and he said, "Now, all this makes sense. Good luck, and have a Merry Christmas." And I thought to myself, *Believe me, you wouldn't believe the 'Mary' Christmas we were going to have.*

The next stop is the Shining Star antique store, or, as Red called it, Mary's Freedom Stop.

Before we all went in, I said, "We have forgotten something significant in all our hustle and bustle and excitement about the delivery and all of its implications. Do either of you know what I am talking about?"

They both looked at each other and then, together, shook their heads no. Then Mary's eyes lit up, and she said, "We, my fine partners in crime, have forgotten one significant holiday, Christmas!"

"You, my fine wife, are so right," I said as I pulled out my wallet. "Here is 120 dollars, 60 dollars apiece for each of you to buy two presents for each of us to be stuck under the tree. The Christmas tree: that we will cut down on the way home. I know of one that will be perfect, and it is going to be taken out by the county this year anyway because it is infringing on the road right of way."

"Now, to make it clear, just because you're 'women.' (And boy, did I get a look from both of them for that statement). Red will buy for Mary and me. Mary will buy it for Red and me, and I will finally buy it for you two. Make it two gifts each, around $15 each, and the sixty should cover each of your purchases. We will use the lights and the angel from last year's tree, and I slyly picked up some paper, bows, and ribbon at the hardware store so that we can be set. Not bad, again, for a 'man'!" I exclaimed.

"Okay, you are right, again, but don't let it go to your head, Mr. Joe!" said Red, as everyone laughed.

I had a few pieces in mind for Fr. John's spinner, and as we walked in, right behind the door was the centerpiece I was looking for. It was a wall table with four stools. The table was all hardwood, rock maple, I think, with a nice, now somewhat hidden, swirled grain.

The stools were a bonus, as they could act as support stands for various spinners. I was in seventh heaven and just barely in the store. I bartered a price for the table and stools as well, and they were in the truck in a flash. Then, I started looking for what would be the focal point of Fr. John's spinner. If I could even find something close to what I had in mind, it would make my day.

As I moved to the back of the store, I found the piece I needed: not just one that would work, but the last, most important piece I needed. It was an old brass book holder with a brass book open on it, which was, and I really couldn't believe it, the Bible. Fr. John's spinner just came to life in my mind.

The girls already had a cart of stuff and seemed as pleased with their finds as I was with mine. At that point, the ladies were ready to roll. I bargained with the clerk and got an excellent deal. It was not a great deal, but there was nothing to complain about, considering all the weird stuff we bought.

The deal included stuff for presents, and I didn't even know what the stuff was, so I guess all in all, I think it was a good deal, no matter what. We put all the things in the truck, and we were ready to head home.

Then, being somewhat 'devious,' I suggested that we drive by the high school where Mary fell in love with me in the first place. First came the blush, a full-on red blush, and then the punch to my ribs.

Which I admit I did deserve, but damn, women can hit hard when they have a solid motivation to do so! It knocked the breath right out of me. Red damn near died laughing and said, "If anyone deserved that, it was you." She shook Mary's hand as both of them stuck their tongues out at me and laughed even more. And even though I could barely breathe, I joined in. As we headed home, we stopped and cut the Christmas tree and threw it into the back of the truck.

I opened the barn doors, and we all piled out and looked at all the stuff we had accumulated in a relatively short time. We took the tree out of the truck along with the other 'new' wind spinner stuff and put it all in the barn. Then we pulled out all the presents we got, took them to the house, and hid them from the receiving party to be wrapped at a later point.

After doing the 'present hiding' thing, we headed back out to the barn. We looked at all the spinner piles, then at the pile of antique store 'finds,' and after much debate and a few actual arguments, we decided to leave the disputed items until last, or at least near last, for an ultimate decision and agreement to be made. At that point, I think everything was pretty much separated and identified, except the disputed pieces.

And I said, "Ladies, good work! I am glad to see both of you still alive." I got a smile from both of them on that comment. Then I went on, "The easy part is the basic 'spinner' work. The tricky part is where the creative part kicks in. And that, my partners, is where the actual artwork begins!

They both looked at the piles of basic junk and knew an art form of their making would come from each pile. They both looked at me, and Mary said, "I know we can do it, but you are the craftsman, and as such, we will definitely need your help, especially for the first couple. Can we count on you?"

I said, "I wouldn't have it any other way. The spinners are all from 'us' to 'them,' but . . .? I might have to be persuaded with a shot, or maybe two, along the way. Deal?"

Mary smiled and looked at Red, who rolled her eyes and shook her head. They both said, "Yes, deal."

By this time, with the sun going down, along with the thermometer, we decided to start first thing in the morning. Mary said, "Well, Joe, 'starting' tomorrow morning, it is your job to come out and get a fire going and warm up the place so we could work without worrying about frostbite since they would be getting breakfast."

I said, "My pleasure, weaklings. I have to feed the horses and dogs anyway since it's way too cold for you two to come out of your pleasantly warm kitchen."

Again, I got the tongues and laughter, and we shut down the barn and went into the house. Knowing we had a lot of work ahead of us, but that we made significant inroads in the 'battle of the spinners' today. A glass of wine and a few shots later, we had some dinner, watched a little TV, and hit the sack because tomorrow would be a long and challenging day.

We started with an early breakfast and threw some snacks into a new basket since the other one was, let me say, in tatters, spread over a wide area by our 'picnic' visitors. I had already been out as they cooked, fed every animal, and had a good fire going.

Red and Mary decided to attack Red's leading central spinner first. It would be made with coconut halves, each with an ancient Anasazi symbol in red. Although the Navajo had a somewhat diverse form of written language, no official standard was universally accepted. So, to Red, the ancient symbols of the Anasazi worked for her, and it was her spinner, as she was proud to say.

Mary and Red started a short assembly line, with Red scraping off the coconut hair off each half they had, which was twenty, with a couple to spare, just in case. Mary scraped out any residual old coconut and then brushed the inside of each shell with Spar varnish to seal against the weather for a waterproof spinner cup. Before we even started, I said, "No gloves, no goggles, no project. We are not losing any fingers or eyes on wind spinners."

I went to work on my first project, Fr. John's Spinner. Emptying the box of chalices onto my workbench, I came up with sixteen silver chalices and four made of hardwood. I didn't have a plan for the wooden ones yet, but again, as my mom always said, 'if needed, God would provide.

Focusing my attention on the silver chalices, I decided to mount them on four wooden wheels, with four chalices per wheel. The wheel/

chalice combination would have to be balanced to spin in the wind. With the silver chalices ranging in size from large to small and in weight from heavy to light, it would take time and ingenuity on my part to make it work.

I preliminarily divided the various silver chalices into what I hoped would be four balanced groups. I took each chalice's cup size and weight as the determining factors. Then, to get an approximate weight of each chalice. I used an old grocery produce scale, where I found it was a mystery. The scale wasn't accurate enough for this project, but it was good enough to start.

While I was puzzling out the chalice problem, the ladies were making good time on the first step of their project. All of the coconuts were basically shaved, scraped, varnished inside, and dried in front of the fire, with the first of the twenty quite dry already.

Then, their next step was to take hand sanders and finish the outside down to a smooth surface on which the spar varnish would be applied in the next step. The coconuts really didn't want to be sanded as smoothly as needed. So, with that said, they took out hand-sanding blocks and hand-sanded each one to a presentable smoothness for the varnish. Although it took time, it worked. By the end of the day, all the coconuts were given a final coat of varnish and were slowly drying in front of the fire to be the ladies' starting point tomorrow.

My project was challenging. I had to balance the spinner wheels with different-weight chalices. Then, I thought of a simple but efficient solution: Plumber's lead left over from the plumbing of the bathroom in my bedroom.

Then, using my bullet maker gas heater to melt the lead. I added the melted lead to each one via a scale weight, so they weren't exactly perfect, but they were damn near perfect. To myself, I thought. *Damn good work, damn good.*

And look at the ladies. They looked like peacocks strutting around their coconuts, and I said, "Ladies, I think we have made excellent progress for the first day. All my chalices weigh almost the same, so they should rotate evenly even in a low wind, just like yours. I will add a little bit more wood to the fire and bank it back so it will stay nice and warm through the night, and your varnish should be as hard as a rock by tomorrow morning."

That said, "I think we should call it a day. I will be in the house in a few after taking care of the fire and making sure everyone here is good to go food-wise, and then I will be right behind you. And to think, we all were so busy we didn't even touch the snacks, which should be just fine tomorrow. And now that the first, and always the most challenging step, has been taken, tomorrow should be even better.

So off you go and check the TV to see what the weather has in store for us tomorrow, and wait for me to celebrate, if you know what I mean. And as we celebrate, we can outline the steps we should take tomorrow. I know my project for Fr. John will probably take at least three days, maybe four, but not any more than that. Tomorrow, you two need to pick out one of the stools to be your spinner's base since it will stand alone out in the middle of the garden. Drill a half-inch hole in the center of the top to support the center spinner shaft. Then, pick your paint, give it an excellent overall coat, and let it dry in front of the fire.

Your next and most demanding task of the day will be to attach the coconuts to the bicycle wheels. Four wheels need to be drilled first for five holes each and then painted. And once the coconuts are connected to the wheels, you ladies will be well on your way to completing your first wind spinner by tomorrow evening." The ladies shook hands and headed into the house with big smiles on their faces.

I hurried, like no one's business, and was in the house in about ten or so minutes, and of course Red goes,

"Thirsty, were we?" "Why, yes," I said. "It was relatively dry in that barn all day. It must have been the warmer weather, along with the warm, dry barn. I can't for the life of me think of any other reason, can you?"

Red goes, "Why yes, I think I can, but we will use your excuse, as it seems to 'work,'" as she hands me a shot. *Well,* I thought, *as I downed that shot, and not having any all day, it hit bottom and hit it hard. But damn, it felt good after a perfect day of, well, thinking and thinking about just how to make something as simple as a wind spinner. It had a calming effect on all of us. The girls were in the kitchen chatting away as if they didn't have a care in the world. And it really made me happy. A deep-down happiness we all needed.*

For a somewhat simple dinner, Red served sliced slow-baked ham with honey and coarse brown sugar glaze and a casserole I taught Red how to make. The casserole is basically asparagus and white onion. The asparagus, drizzled with olive oil, is baked in a 400-degree oven for about twenty minutes until it is just tender.

Then, you take a nice firm, pungent white onion, cut it into rings, and layer the rings on the asparagus. Drizzle additional garlic-flavored olive oil on the onion, and broil at 425 degrees until the onions start to lightly brown. Pull out of the oven, sprinkle with a generous handful of shredded mozzarella cheese, and continue baking until the cheese melts down into the onions.

Then, it comes out of the oven, and four nice dollops of sour cream are placed on top, drizzled with chunky blue cheese dressing, and served. It is fantastic if I do say so myself, since it is my recipe. Then, a cubed cucumber and tomato salad with the same blue cheese dressing. What can I say?

We all ate well and sat down to discuss tomorrow. To the ladies, I said, "Your assignment, should you choose to accept it, will be the following."

1. I figured four tiers with five coconuts on each tier, each tier turning in the opposite direction. This would mean four painted bike wheels, your choice of bright colors, all the same or different for each level. Each spinner can be a single color from the others; it's your choice. Then paint and let all four dry well, then apply a quick second coat.

2. Each wheel will require a five-hole pattern, which is basically a star. Use markers to lay out your star on one so it is balanced, drill it, and then drill the other three the same. (Touch up the holes so they don't rust out, or drill before you paint. Again, it's your choice.)

3. While they are drying, drill a hole in the side of each coconut. Use glue and a clamp to hold the coconut in place. I have at least ten clamps to use, and the glue should set in about thirty minutes.

4. Your center spinner will be on a long piece of rebar since it is in the middle of the garden. Each of your levels should be about eight

inches or so apart, so you will need about an eight-foot piece of rebar for your center spinner. We can stick the rebar in the dirt floor area of the barn, near the fireplace, and paint the symbols there.

My work for tomorrow is centered on four tasks:

1. Paint my wooden wheels silver with four holes in each wheel.

2. Paint my candle holders silver as well.

3. My chalices are going to be attached four to a wheel. But instead of aligning them sideways, they will face forward and backward. Thus, not only the wind but also the rain will cause them to turn. Each of the wheels will be mounted in tandem on either side of a candlestick. The candlesticks will then be attached to each side of the wall table, sort of like a Ferris wheel.

4. I will first use my belt sander to do the primary sanding on the table since it is all square wood with no curves to deal with. Then, I will hand sand to a good, smooth finish, but not one I would do for indoor furniture, especially since it will be outside. I figure that should take about a maximum of two hours.

After a thorough wipe down to remove dust, I intend to apply red teak spar varnish, hopefully, two coats tomorrow and one the next day. On the third day, I will apply a heavy clear coat of spar varnish very early, let it dry basically to the touch, and then start attaching the two Ferris wheel spinners with the brass book/Bible holder in between. I looked closely at it, and it was made to be outside, on a grave maker.

"And, my fair ladies," I said, "during my downtime of drying and such, I would love to work with both of you in any way I can help. Because, as Smokey and the Bandit say, 'We've got a long way to go and a short time to get there'!"

"Red," I said in a harsh, raspy voice, "All this talking has taken my voice plum away. Would you have any medicine that might work on this poor soul's throat?" Red thinks for a minute or so and says, "No medicine that I can think of except . . . maybe say a nice shot? That is, if Ms. Mary had a little wine and poor little old me had a shot as well, I think everyone would feel much better, especially Mary's ears and mine as well!"

"Red, you're just a soul of generosity, did you know that?" I said, still harsh and raspy. As Red delivered, I said, "God bless you, child." But Mary was really getting good with that pillow. She hit me square in the head but didn't even come close to the shot. I said, "God bless you as well, child. I see your aim has improved. Although close, no drop was spilled. Can I hear an 'amen,' sisters?"

Red says, "I'd watch out for lightning if I were you, Mary!"

Everybody was tired, and the beds were waiting. "Good nights" were said by everyone. Mary and I were in bed, snuggled together, and asleep within minutes. I lasted just a little longer and thought, I'll *get up early and quietly make a pot of coffee. Then, head out to the barn and get the fire up and going, which shouldn't take much because of the banked coals and fire already there. Alfalfa for the horses and a conglomerate of dog food and scraps were devoured by the dogs, and I would be ready to start. I would leave a note for the ladies to bring me a roll with ham and a 'special' cup of coffee"* as they headed out to the barn. *Then, like the others, sleep took me.*

CHAPTER TEN

I rolled over, and it was five, so I quietly got up and executed my plan. Within twenty minutes, I had the band sander working on the finish, and to my surprise, within, say, ten to fifteen minutes, the rough sanding was done, and the hand sanding had begun. What I discovered was that this table was a magnificent work of some craftsman. The rock maple had a beautiful, swirled grain throughout the top, the sides, and all the way through each leg.

If it weren't to be used for Fr. John's spinner, I would have kept it for myself. And again, the smooth hand sanding, considering the hardness of the wood, was almost like magic. Next came the first coat of the red teak-colored spar varnish applied top to bottom and underneath, and I moved it over to the fire pit to dry. What had been a discarded old table became a work of art as the red varnish caught the glow of the fire as it dried. Red and Mary came in from the house, and Mary said, "I felt you get up, but I fell back asleep and didn't know you were out here. What have you accomplished while we were sleeping the morning away?"

I smiled, pointed to the table, and said, "Just that." Both of their expressions were of wonder as they examined the table. Red handed me my roll and special coffee and said, "Joe, you deserve this. That table is beautiful!" Thanks, I said, "It really came together quicker than I thought, and if I hadn't already had plans for it! It would be in our house, I guarantee."

"I agree," said Mary, "and that is just the first coat of the red teak-colored spar varnish. I can't wait to see the final product." "And, ladies,"

I said, "I figured out how to balance your five coconuts on your wheel. "Mary, please grab five of your coconuts and a wheel. And Red, grab that piece of plywood over by the east wall, and you shall see. It should take a few minutes, you two, so be ready to be amazed at how easy it actually is."

Mary went and got the coconuts and the wheel, and Red grabbed the plywood. "Okay," I said, "you have five coconuts to attach to a circle, so you have to have a star pattern, and this is how you do it."

"Oh, and Mary, there is a marker over on the bench where I am working. Please bring it here," I said. "Because once we get them laid in position, we mark each center, and we have a pattern for the other three."

Using the wheel as a pattern, I drew a circle. Then, I placed one coconut at the top and, working around the circle, put the other four in the right places.

Then, over on the side of the board, I drew the star we needed, and then we started using the same directional flow I did with the picture to move each coconut to its position. Within minutes and some relatively minor adjustments, the star was balanced in the circle.

They were both amazed as they looked from every side and agreed it worked. Red said, "You continue to amaze me with how you think of stuff. I am thinking you might have a little help from you know who, the Good Guy upstairs."

They marked the center of each coconut on the board, laid each wheel on the board, and marked it. Without further ado, they drilled the holes and started painting. Choosing the paint was their problem, so I turned my attention to the table.

I touched the top, and it was ready for the second coat. And if I were to venture a guess, it should bring out the deep-swirled grain even more. The second coat flowed on much easier than the first since it wasn't being brushed on raw wood. I placed the table back by the fire to dry, with my subsequent task being the chalices. Attaching the chalices to the wheels was pretty easy overall. Especially since there were only four chalices per wheel, and they were all cleaned and sprayed with clear varnish yesterday. I attached the chalices to the wheels. Then,

I mounted two wheels to each candlestick tee, and they were ready with bearings in place. They spun quickly without a heavy spot to slow down the movement on any of the four.

The book/Bible stand came predrilled, so all I did yesterday was polish it up and apply a coat of spar varnish. With that done, I was waiting on the table and its last heavy coat of clear spar varnish. Father's spinner would be done in record time.

With Fr. John's spinner almost finished, I turned my attention to the next spinner to be built. I asked the ladies for their opinions on the matter. They surveyed the spinner piles, and Mary said, "The one made up of the wooden Dutch shoes would be a real test of skill." As I thought to myself, *I was afraid they would say that one.*

I went to the pile in question and organized all the 'stuff' into a somewhat logical order. Then I walked around the barn looking for the missing puzzle piece to pull all the 'stuff' together. I wasn't sure what the piece was, but I was sure I would know it when I saw it.

As I was looking, I remembered my special coffee and ham roll sandwich that the ladies had laid by the fire to keep warm. With my coffee and sandwich in hand, I said, "Thanks, this will definitely help me think."

I pulled up one of the unpainted stools, sipped my exceptional coffee," and ate that ham and roll with hot spicy mustard, just like I liked it. And it hit the spot.

Thinking to myself as I took my last swallow of special coffee, I remembered something that might be my missing puzzle piece. Within minutes, I had the item I had thought of and showed it to the ladies. They both looked askance at a black metal, circular staircase I had in my hands. It was designed for a single person to have access to, say, an attic crawl space.

Then I said, "Now you will see a real master craftsman at work." The staircase had ten adjustable steps on a central pole. This allowed me to adjust the steps to complete the wind circle, which meant that when the bottom shoe was finished with the wind, the top one was starting, with all the others following suit.

To complete the ten steps, I would need ten shoes, and I had eleven. I already had a use for shoe number eleven in my head. *Perfect*, I thought to myself. So, I got out my cutting torch and went to work.

Of the separated piles, I found five bicycle fenders, which, when cut in half, made ten. And then, for the top, was a little metal Dutch flag, which Margie had found the day we were there. I used a hack saw to cut the five fenders in half, and I drilled three holes in all of the ten fender halves at once so they would be pretty much uniform. I spray painted three red, three white, and three blue, and the last one white, red, and blue. Which are the colors of the Dutch Flag. Then I went to work on the stairs.

I cut the handrail off in segments between the steps, leaving just enough on each step to attach a shoe. Then, using one of the fenders as a guide, I marked each step with drill and cut marks. Then out came the drill, followed closely by my torch, and each step was drilled and cut the same. Then, I repainted the steps black, precisely where they had been cut. I let everything dry while I went and finished my coffee.

Then, being a gentleman, I asked the ladies, since I was going to the house, if they wanted anything. Red spoke up, "Special coffee," and then Mary, "Wine, please, and since you are there, two more rolls and ham for Red and me." "Got it," I said and went to the house.

I came back with three rolls, two special cups of coffee, and wine. You ladies didn't peak at my Dutch shoe spinner, did you? "No, actually," Red said, "we are up to our asses in coconuts and bicycle wheels. Whose idea was it to choose this spinner? Oh yes, it was me! Why this one was stupid, or shall I say, ridiculous is a closer description!" Mary asked, "So, how is the Dutch shoe spinner coming?"

"Fair at this point. Still working on a few bugs," I said. Mary rolled her eyes and said, "I'll bet money he almost has it done," she said to Red. "No doubt," said Red as she went back to attaching a coconut.

I went back to all the stuff that I sprayed varnish on, and they were dry. The spar spray varnish came out again and finished all those pieces up. Then I walked over to the table, and it was dry, so the heavy clear spar varnish coat was ready to go on. Like the second coat, it went smoothly and fast, and the table was drying by the fire within ten minutes. With any luck, in an hour or so, it would be dry to the touch, just like I wanted it to be. That way, the pieces would not only be attached with the screws but would adhere to the surface itself.

The ladies had just attached the last of the coconuts to the four wheels and had just sat down to a sandwich and wine or coffee as I brought the table over to the fireplace to dry. And I said, "At this point, I think Santa might hire us next year, since we are just a little busy this year, to join his elves."

"You've got to be kidding. If I ever want another spinner, please just shoot me," said Red as Mary goes, "If he doesn't, I will."

We all relaxed for about a half hour. Then I went over to Red and said, "Here, let me show you how to attach the spacers to the rebar so we can get an idea of how it is going to look." Red says, "Fine." I went to get the rebar and attached the first level, and Mary said, "That shouldn't be too hard."

And then Red says sarcastically, "That's what I said about the coconuts in the first place, remember?"

Mary just shook her head, yes, but then said, "I know we can do it, so let's just do it, okay?"

Red smiles and says, "Yes, we can do it; even Joe could do it, at least I think he could."

As they both laugh at my expense. I just smiled and thought, *Wait until they see the Dutch shoe spinner.*

I better get back to work and put it all together, and I hope it works. No, I have faith it will. And it did, right down to the 11th shoe with the Dutch flag sticking in it for the crowning top piece.

Now, let's see how dry the table is. As I walked over to it, it was tacky and dry, just like I wanted. I carefully carried it back to my workshop area and placed the book/Bible holder in the faint marks I put on the table just before the last coat and then screwed it down. Then again, in the faint marks, I attached both of the teed candle sticks with the reverse Ferris wheel chalices. Then I went out and pounded a piece of rebar into the dirt floor by the fireplace.

Red says, "So, mister, what may that piece of rebar be for?" I said, "You shall see magic in a matter of minutes!"

The ladies decided to take a bathroom break at this point because, according to Mary, I was being too 'high and mighty.'

While they were gone, I took the Dutch shoe spinner and slid it on the rebar. Next came Fr. John's completed wind spinner. And if I may say so, they both were, at least, adorable. But anyway, they both needed time in front of the fire to bake on the final coat of spar varnish. And, maybe, to show off both of my projects, just a wee bit, to my coconspirators in the 'wind spinner initiative.'

The ladies came back in after using the bathroom; they stopped in their tracks and just started at the two actual works of art drying in front of the fireplace. They both walked over and examined each piece in detail, and Red gently spun the Dutch shoe tree. Red said, "You are truly a master craftsman, and you really have my utmost respect, and I do mean it. They are both, really, works of art."

Mary, not to be undone, said, "Joe, you could get hundreds, no maybe even thousands of dollars for each one of those. They are truly magnificent."

I said, blushing profusely, "Thanks, it is just what comes out of me when I put my mind to a project. That's all, nothing more, nothing less."

And as they both give me a big hug, I say, "Well, ladies, the rest are a lot simpler and should go together quickly. At least let's hope so, for our sanity's sake." Looking at both of them, I said, "We still have four days until Doc and Margie get here for Mary's exam and dinner, and I would like to have all, if not most, of the others done by then. So, what do you say? Do you think we can all pull it off?"

Mary says, "With your help, my love, I have no doubt. What do you think, Red?"

Red says, "Yes, I think we really can get them done. We still have a few hours left today, and we basically have the three hardest ones done. The rest are cups, plastic glasses, some small wooden windows, and such. It will be quite a bit of work, but it is doable. So, 'yes,' I say again. We can do it."

Over the next four days, the three of us turned seven piles of junk into seven wind spinners, which the owners will be proud to have in their gardens or yards this spring.

Doc and Margie showed up right at six, as they said they would. The first thing Margie said was, "What a beautiful Christmas tree. Where on earth did you find the time to put it up? On top of that, it's a real one." She gave Marc a scathing look and said, "Ours is still in the garage!"

To change the subject quickly, Doc goes, "Mary's exam is the first thing on the docket. 'Mary, you are wanted in exam room no. 1, now make it quick, I am running behind," he said with a smile.

And I think, even though I shouldn't be, I worry through every exam, every time. Red knows, hands me a shot, and says, "It all will be well. You can count on it." I smile and swallow the shot. About fifteen minutes later, Doc and Mary walk out smiling, and I can stop holding my breath again.

Doc says, "Fit as a fiddle, and if I were a betting man, I would bet, labor on the twenty-fourth, and birth on the twenty-fifth. That is, if I were a betting man. Now, what's for dinner?"

"We will get to that in a minute," I say to Doc and Margie. "We want to show you what we have been busting our tails off on for the last week or so. And to tell the truth, it started as a way to kill time until birth, and it almost killed us. So come on out to the barn. Just grab your jackets; the barn is warm, and you will see why when you get there." Then, with everyone in tow, we headed to the barn, where Mary and Red were barely able to contain themselves.

I open the doors as everyone hurries in and quickly close them again to keep the heat in. Margie and Doc basically stop in their tracks, and Margie says, "You guys did all of this in little over a week? How could you? Did the elves come down? And she goes, and the shoes. Those are the Dutch shoes. Marc, can you believe all of this, and on top of all of it, our shoes? As she went over and gingerly spun it, tears of joy flowed down her cheeks.

Marc asked, "Who did this? It is an amazing work of art, too good for a garden."

Then Mary chimes in and says, "We just happen to have a master craftsman in our mist. My husband Joe designed and built 'your' spinner out of his head and his heart for you two. We all hope you like it."

Margie, still crying, gave me a bear hug of love for a man at this point second only to her husband and said, "You truly deserve the name of Joseph, as 'Joseph' was a master craftsman as well and was chosen by God, just like you were." And the only thing Marc could say was, "I couldn't have said it any better myself. And look at all the other works of art. I have a feeling that God's hands were in this barn all week, and of that, I have no doubt. And Red and Mary, I can see your spirits in every other piece in here.

Except for one other that I am sure Joe did just for Fr. John: the table with the brass Bible and the chalices. That was also just your work, wasn't it, Joe?"

"Yes, I wanted it to be his special Christmas present, well, besides Mary's two gifts, which truly dwarf anything a man like me could ever do."

"Now," I said, "let's go eat, and I think a shot or two and a glass of wine or so are in order if that is okay with everyone. All of the spinners still need a few days to be hard enough to withstand the weather around here. Plus, it had been a long, challenging, and thirsty day if I say so myself, and with that said, everyone into the house."

Margie walked back over to their spinner and said, "I agree with Marc; this will be 'in' our home."

As everyone headed toward the house, I was the last one out. I looked up, crossed myself, and said, "Thanks!" Then, I banked the fire and closed the barn doors since everyone had already been fed earlier.

As the meal was over and Doc and Margie were leaving, Doc said, "Mary, I will be back around the twenty-first for your final checkup. It will be more just for the final setup for the delivery, what to expect, and what we will need in the way of supplies, especially since this is going to be a home birth. I will have all I need, but I will make a list of the needed general supplies for Joe and Red. Do you have any questions?"

Mary hesitates and says, "Only a million or so, but I trust in God and in your skill that all will be as it should be. But thanks for asking."

As we all walk out into the night, the sky is ablaze with falling stars. Red goes, "Well, look at that! If that isn't a good sign, I can't think of one." Then I pipe up and say, "That, my fine woman, is the peak of the Geminids Meteor shower. The most brilliant of each year and getting more so every year due to the main asteroid, Phaethon, 'mother' of the shower itself, wobbling and getting closer and closer to the sun on each rotation. Therefore, more pieces are breaking away to enter our atmosphere. And that again, my fine woman, is your science lesson for the day and an excellent sign. God gave us a crystal-clear night to view it.

And just so you also know, there is a lessor shower named Ursid, which peaks around December 24. This should generate somewhat of a diversion, just in case Mary causes a 'distraction' in the universe herself with the birth of the twins. Everyone is quiet for a moment and then says good night. The three of us go into the house and stand in front of the fire to warm up.

Then Mary quietly asks me, "Do you really think that the birth will cause a 'universal distraction,' as you said?" I thought for a moment, take Mary into my arms, and say, "Yes, I think so. Just think about the three wise men and the star. But I also think, for some reason, and my reasoning has been pretty good lately, that 'he' has a distraction of his own, besides the Ursid meteor shower, to keep 'you know who' very busy. So, relax, and as I figure, it is in God's hands at this point."

The ladies headed for bed after a very long day, which was the end of a very long week, in which we accomplished what could only be called a 'miracle' to get all those spinners done in record time. Sure, we had some minor stuff to do yet, but overall, we had pretty much completed the 'spinner" project.' As Mary walked toward the bedroom, I said, "I'll be in in a minute or so. I want to sit here and relax a bit. You can join me if you would like?"

Mary says, "No, I know you have been under stress that would kill an ordinary man, so you need a little quiet time to yourself. Take as long as you need, but kiss me as you come to bed so I know that you are there. That is one of the most important things in my life now and forever more, my love. Good night." She closes the bedroom door, gets ready for bed, climbs in, and drops into a deeply deserved sleep.

I felt terrible for a bit for not going directly to bed with Mary, but thought to myself, *She was right; I do need a moment, well hell more like, well I really don't know, but a few minutes will have to do!*

I went to the kitchen, turned on the hot water, let it run, grabbed a snifter and a bottle of whiskey, and poured a moderately full glass, being a small snifter. Then, I filled a glass with boiling water, walked over to the easy chair by the fireplace, placed the snifter on the hot water, and let it warm.

As I let the warmth of the fire bake into me. I glanced at the snifter, and it was warm and steamy, so I picked it up and let the fragrance of the whiskey tease my nose. Then I took a deep sip and swirled it with my tongue, then let it slowly slide down my throat as I thought, *You know God, which I am sure you do, the asteroid we humans named Phaethon is in a wobbly orbit and getting closer and closer to the sun as it also is to earth. And if, let's say, a sizable 'piece' of it entered our atmosphere, just saying, mind you, and hit a real bastion of hell on earth, such as, for example, the Sinaloa Cartel in Culiacan, Mexico. I would think that the Prince's mind just might be more than a little distracted at the birthing time, wouldn't you think? Just a suggestion.*

I smiled to myself despite being just a little, well, more than a little, a lot sacrilegious, but I felt better thinking it than not. My bed and a beautiful woman, my wife no less, sleeping in it beckoned to me strongly. I finished the snifter, put it in the kitchen, and headed to bed. I made sure to kiss her as I snuggled in beside her and fell into a well-deserved, deep, and restful sleep.

The following day, Doc called with a list of supplies we would need on our end. While I was in town getting supplies, I drove by Jose's, now with a new sign calling the diner Sam's and a grand opening date of January 5 on the door.

A new name and new ownership are good signs for the New Year. Then, just in case, I stopped by the liquor store and got some more whiskey and a bottle of good champagne to celebrate when the time came, which, without a doubt, would be early Christmas morning.

Then, I headed home using the backway. Just, well, just because as I passed Jim's, I waved out the window because he would know two things. One, nothing had happened, or he would have heard immediately, and second, the camera was watching my every move, and it let Jim know all was 'okay' at the Everlasting Ranch.

As I pulled up, Doc's truck was outside the barn, and he and Margie were carefully loading the wind spinner into the back of the truck. I hurried over and helped, and before I could say a word, Margie said, "Yes, this was my idea. I wanted it in the house for Christmas, and since Marc liked the idea and we were going to be here anyway, now seemed like the perfect time. So there."

I said, "No arguments from me. One less I have to deliver. Here, I will help you tie it down. I have some spare bungee cords in the barn that should do the trick." Within minutes, we were done, and they were headed into the house. I grabbed all the stuff I bought and brought it in to have Marc make sure that he had everything he needed from their end. After a quick scan, Marc gave his okay and took the stuff into the bedroom that he needed, leaving the rest in the kitchen that Red would require when the time came.

Red offered a meal, but they declined. Mary's exam went very well, which was expected. But Margie was looking at the clouds on the edge of the ridge and said to Marc, "Let's get going; I want that spinner in the house before the snow starts." And off they went.

And now we were down to about two and a half days, and Mary showed it. Being a man, I really didn't know how large a woman just about to give birth to twins could be or how uncomfortable and irritable she could also be.

As she walked out of the room, her first words were, "I need a glass of wine now, maybe two. I haven't had any today, so I am entitled. Right!" Red already had one in hand and said, "Right you are! Here, enjoy, and the second one is already poured!" Mary sheepishly said, "Sorry, I didn't mean to be a little, I mean, as she patted her stomach, a big bitch, but it just came out. Both of you, please forgive me."

"There's no need to forgive; we probably don't understand, but we do feel for you from the bottom of our hearts. Right, Red!" I said. Red said, "I couldn't have said it better. Now, you sit back and try to relax while we two mortals try to come up with some supper." That brought a big smile to Mary's face, and she said, "Mortals, my ass!" And everyone laughed as the tension left the room.

Just then, Doc came sliding up in his truck and jumped out with a box covered with a blanket. He knocked on the door, rushed into the house, and set the box on the floor. Immediately, the sound of small barks emanated from the box. I looked at Doc, and he said, "I can explain."

"About eight, no nine weeks ago, my neighbor's pure-breed golden lab gave birth to a litter of pups sired from a registered male golden lab. And since he knew Mary was giving birth to twins, and that is all he knew, he wanted to give a gift to her and the twins. He reached into the box and said, "But before you say anything, I have already named them, and you will see why I called them as I did.

The first one out of the box was a tough, strong-looking male, and Doc said his name was Stronger. The second, a female, was also a great-looking dog, although leaner, but still with a lab's strength evident. Her name is Compassion. So, my reasoning was really very simple. 'Christian's strength is made 'Stronger' because of Hope's 'Compassion.'"

Mary about died at that point and hugged him. But there still was a muted bark from the box. "And before I introduce the last pup, I have to explain." Doc said, "I have a strong feeling that Stronger will gravitate to Christian and Compassion to Hope very soon, if not immediately like Coal and Snow did. I also feel that Coal will switch allegiance to Joe, Snow, and Mary. And Red, this last pup, although the runt of the litter, is yours and yours alone."

He handed him to her, and she cried like a baby. Holding the dog close to her breast, she actually kissed him full on the lips and said, "God bless you, you wonderful man. You have made my dreams come true, I swear. And I shall name him Sly, after my husband. Who was as smart as can be but just a little on the small side himself. Thank you, thank you, and thank you! I know in my heart I can't say it enough, but I think a shot for three and a glass for two might do it."

Marc says, "Well, I think that just might do it. That is, if you insist."

"I insist," said Red. And we all drank a toast to what else but "to the dogs." Stronger and Compassion were put on the floor, and sure enough, he curled up next to Coal, and she curled up next to Snow.

Marc said, "What'd I tell you? Oh, and they are all potty trained and eat dry dog food just like yours, so they should be right at home. Well, I've got to go. Margie's worried about the storm, and I think she should be. But Mary, I will be here no matter if I have to come by snowmobile. Got it?" She just shook her head yes as he headed out of the door. And then I said, "Oh, Mary, one thing that I have never told you. . . Was that if push comes to shove, I have delivered two babies in the bush of Nam, so I do know what to do, just in case." And then Red piped in and said, "I delivered my niece in the back of a pickup truck in the middle of winter, on the way to the hospital, without a single hitch. So, no matter what, you are in good hands, either to help or, as Joe said if push comes to shove, you are covered."

Mary ran to the two of us, hugged us tightly, and said, "Thank you. I always knew I could depend on you two no matter what."

CHAPTER ELEVEN

Well, even if it seemed like forever, the twenty-fourth finally rolled around. And even with a storm blowing outside, Doc and Margie were at the door at eight in the morning, as promised, with Fr. John at their side. Doc was there at eight just in case the storm got worse, and Margie was there to hold Mary's hand and mine if needed.

Fr. John looked at their tree and said how beautiful it was. And then he said, "Especially, the angel. It looks almost ancient." "Well," I said, "it has been in the family for generations and originally had a candle to light it, but it was replaced with wire decades ago. And when I got it, I upgraded it to better wiring, so I guess you could call it ancient, or at least an ancient antique passed down through generations to the oldest son or daughter if there wasn't a son in that generation.

But I find it beautiful, and every year, I put it on a tree. And then I'm sad when I take it off after Christmas to be put away for another year. It is hand-blown glass. And as the story goes, it was made by a monk in Italy a very long time ago."

Then I looked around and said to everyone, "Since we have time to wait, I want to show Fr. John his Christmas present. If you all would bundle up, we are headed to the barn."

Fr. John, with his focus totally on Mary and the babies, really didn't want to go. But knowing that they did have time to wait, in fact, quite a bit of time, he put his jacket back on, and they all took on the storm and hurried to the barn.

Earlier in the day, I had moved the other spinners to the side so that they could still be seen and admired, but I set the table directly in front of the fireplace, and it had a fire slowly burning behind the table. Fr. John was the last one in, as he really didn't want to miss a minute of today and tonight. But since everyone else was going, he went. As he came out of the storm, the crowd of people parted, and there in front of him was his spinner. And I said, "Merry Christmas, Father."

Fr. John just stood there, frozen with emotion. He slowly walked over to the table and ran his hand gently across the top of the table, walked around it, and looked at it like a blind man with sight for the first time. He looked at me with tears welling up in his eyes and said, "You built this for me? Joe, it is not only a beautiful creation but a magnificent tribute to God. I can't . . ." "Father, it is okay, I understand. I am sure I had help, as everything I needed fell into my lap, and it was just up to me to make it the best I could to honor God and you. I hope you like it as much as I think you do?" I asked.

"Like it, like it? Joe, it is a work of art. You have earned the name of 'Joseph.' You, like your namesake, are/were craftsmen of your times," said Fr. John.

I said, "I think I have heard that lately," as I looked at Mary and Red and smiled. I continued, "We will drop it off after Christmas, but I just couldn't wait any longer for you to see it. Let's go back in and wait patiently, yeah, right, for the babes to arrive."

Fr. John was the last to leave, as he had to take at least one more look. Then he remembered why he was here and hurried out as I closed the barn doors after stirring up the coals and throwing an additional log on the fire.

With everyone back in the house, Marc stretched out on the couch after one shot of whiskey, anticipating a long night. I had a shot of whiskey myself, sat down in the easy chair, put my feet up on the ottoman, and promptly took a snooze as well. Red, Mary, Margie, and Fr. John played Monopoly in the kitchen. Then, about 6:00 p.m., Mary had her first contraction, and the delivery was on. Margie, being a nurse, noted the time so they could keep track of the contractions as they increased in frequency and strength.

Everyone except Mary was calm at this point. That is if you don't count me. I started pacing and really never stopped except to have a couple of sandwiches, and now that it was going to be quite a while yet, a beer or so mixed with the occasional shot. I thought, as the 'father,' it was my prerogative.

Then, around seven, the second and more muscular contraction took place. After that, each contraction was sooner and stronger about every half hour or so. At ten-thirty, Margie got Marc up, and they took Mary into the 'delivery' room and started monitoring her blood pressure on a steady basis from now on.

By eleven, Mary was quite dilated, and both babies were in good positions. But the only one not in a 'good position' was me; I was a nervous wreck. Fr. John wasn't much better, with Red not far behind both of us.

So now, only time will tell. And as I said a month or so ago, 'just as it's Christmas,' the delivery was in total progress. Christian was first at ten after twelve, while Hope followed a close second, being born at twelve after twelve.

And as I heard the second cry, I burst into the room, with Red and the Father right behind me, only to see Mary holding both babies to her breasts, with the biggest smile ever on her face. Fr. John dropped to his knees, crossed himself, and said, "Thank you, God, for letting me be here to witness the birth of your saviors."

I stood there staring at Mary, holding Christian and Hope. I said a silent prayer of thanks to God for the miracle of life. And Mary said, "Joe, I would like you to meet Christian and Hope. Children, I am sure that you know, but this man at the end of my bed gawking at me is your father."

And at that point, I swear they both opened their eyes and looked straight into mine. And then both their eyes closed like it never even happened. Then I said, "Mary, they are beautiful, my wife and now mother." And as I moved to her side and kissed her and gently touched both Christian and Hope, I said, "I didn't think it was possible, but I love you more, damn woman, so much more," as tears of joy streamed down my cheeks.

And then Mary said, "Joe, I'll take that shot of the good stuff now." Marc frowned just a little and said, "Make it three, and then, looking at the crowd, better make it six." Margie just smiled and said, "Yes, make it six. One only gets one chance in a lifetime to see not only one but two saviors born on the same day, within minutes of each other," as she cried tears of joy and thanked God.

And unknown to all of them until the next day. A piece of an asteroid that scientists think came from Phaethon, the Mother of the Geminids meteors, plunged into Earth's atmosphere and almost destroyed the most significant drug cartel in the world, the Sinaloa Cartel, killing over a thousand drug and crime lords at their annual celebration of the anti-Christ in Culiacan, Mexico.

Unknown to all but God himself, The Dark Lord walked away from the carnage alive but very weak and burned severely. He took strength from the souls of the few that survived and recovered enough to return to hell to lick his wounds for another day.

"God," he swore, "you and yours will pay for this! You personally, if I ever get a chance, you will pay the ultimate price. As I take this planet and all the souls on it and make it and them mine!"

As I sat there quietly holding the twins that could save the world one day, a news story on TV caught my attention. It was something about a meteor destroying a drug Cartel in Mexico, and I thought, *Good plan, God! One damn good distraction!*

Both of the babies were asleep, as was Mary. So Red took the babies to the cribs, now in what had been my room and what now seemed like ages ago.

Doc, Margie, and Fr. John called it a day and headed home with strict instructions from Doc, too, "Call if anything, and I do mean anything, comes up."

That just left me and Red to have a couple of shots in front of the fireplace. Sly was in Red's lap like he had been there since the day he was born. I just sat there sipping my whiskey, knowing my life had just changed for what would be both better and worse. Each would come, and I knew it. Strangely, I welcomed it because it had finally started!

And as I thought to myself, *Damn you, Prince of Darkness! Unknown to you, my son and my daughter, together, are going to "Kick Your Ass." And Mary, Red, and I will be there to help them. Mary and I both know if saving God and our children means dying so they can save the world, we will die doing it, plain and simple.*

Red is still unknown. But until our end, we will be by their side, teaching, guiding, loving them, and, most importantly, protecting them with every part of our beings. And please help us, God, because we will need every bit you can spare. Amen!

As I looked at the wolf pelt on the wall, I said to Red, "I have something to tell you about the end if you want to hear it."

Red took a deep breath and said, "Yes."

I say, "Okay, and I tell her about 'Death Walker's' promise as part of the conditions that he would, upon my command, release all the wolves, millions, upon millions, dead, living, or even just moving dust and bones, on the enemy. How that happens, I do not actually know, but if all goes right, it will. And I can't wait until I release the wolves from their king's promise, and they rip into those assholes at the last battle. They'll be more than a little bit shocked, wouldn't you think?"

"That I would, Joe, and I am now looking forward to that last battle so badly. But I also know the price this world is going to have to pay to get to that point. But you know, it will be worth it because the kids, our or ours, and I hope you don't mind me saying ours, they will be the ultimate benefactors. And thank you for telling me that."

"No, Red, I don't mind ours, not at all." Then I said, "We may come to blows over what I will have to do at times, but just remember when it all comes down to it. God put me in charge of their protection, and I will honor that responsibility even if it means my death. Because, if you really want to know, it will! And I know it will, and I think Mary's as well, but that I am not sure of, but mine I am. I don't know if you noticed, but in my vows and Mary's, neither of us said, 'Until death do us part."

Red says, "I did, Joe, and figured as much, and if so, so be it."

And then I said, "But somehow, someway, I, or Mary and I, will be back to finish the job we started. To finish what seems to have started a long time ago, but in reality, was now only a couple or so months ago."

"Joe, I have said this before, and I am sure I will repeat it, 'God picked the right man for the job.'"

With that, Red said, "One more, and then bed. We have a long, difficult life facing us because, like it or not, I am in it with you two for the long haul."

"I know," I said, "and I have always known. And yes, to the shot, and then yes, to bed. The twins are due up in about two or so hours."

Then I said, "Then pour, woman; daylight is just around the corner." We both smiled, clicked our glasses, and drank our shots. We both knew life had just really begun as our respective doors closed, and we each crawled into each of our beds.

I kissed Mary on the back of her neck and said quietly, "Good job, my love!" And I heard a whisper of 'thanks' from Mary. And then I fell asleep, at least for a few hours, because when Mary got up to feed the twins, I was up sitting with her in the living room, just smiling. Knowing after a while, she would bring them back to bed with her while she nursed, but for now, she would be up, and so would I.

When the children were done, I got up and took Hope, Mary took Christian, and we put them in their cradles. They were asleep almost before we covered them up. It was about a quarter after four, so if they stayed asleep until around eight, Mary could feed them. Then we, meaning Red, Mary, and me, could have our Christmas present opening with special coffee and a coffee cake that Red had ready to go into the oven just before she went to bed. So they could eat, drink and merrily open a few presents.

Eight seemed to come way too soon, but babies only know when they are wet and messy and then when they are hungry. And they were all three, and by the time they got to feeding, you would have thought they hadn't eaten in days. Mary was still adjusting to nursing, but in her heart, she knew the pain would quickly diminish, and the pleasure of nursing offset any discomfort in her eyes. After about twenty minutes or so, they slowed down and started to drift off to sleep.

I grabbed Christian, and Red grabbed Hope, and down they went as if it was just what they were supposed to do. Mary, on the other hand, hit the bathroom in a rush from the babies, interrupting the usual start to her day.

Then, everyone quickly drank their coffee and devoured the coffee cake because it was time for presents! Red went first by consensus and opened her first one from me. As she opened it, she was gleefully surprised to find that it was a book on preserving garden fruits and vegetables by sun drying.

Mary was next, and she picked one from me. It was a bright red bird feeder that had been used for almost no time. It still had the tag on it, which I had failed to remove, but she loved it. And gave me a big hug. Then came me. It was a long box from both Red and Mary, and they couldn't wait for me to open it.

I ripped into it like a madman, and much to my utmost surprise, it was an ancient 30-30 Winchester rifle with what looked like original peep sights. The stock was badly scarred and had a long crack in it, but I tried the action, and it was sound, and the barrel was clean and smooth. What a find.

The stock could be refinished, and the crack was along the grain of the wood, and once glued and finished, you would never know it had been split from the barrel end to the butt end of the stock. It seemed like it had been done intentionally, but that made absolutely no sense to me at the time. I could have the metal all refinished for a minimal amount, and it would be like new. I couldn't believe it. I had to ask, "So I know it is rude, but how much?"

Red said proudly, "It is rude, but if you must know, 60 bucks."

I kissed them both and said, "With a few hours of work, it could be worth three to four hundred dollars, easy, or so much more considering the very low serial number on the gun's action." Mary said to Red, "I told you it was a steal at that price, and I was right."

"Honey," I said, "yes, you were!"

"Okay, Mary, you are next." She picked mine again. I don't know why, but she did. Tears filled her eyes as she pulled an apron out of the box. On the front, in big letters, was written, 'Mother Knows Best.'

You would have thought I had given her a diamond ring as she held the apron up and said, "In a month or so, I will quickly be wearing this very proudly.

Then, Red opened one from Mary, a pewter plaque with the words 'World's Best Stepmom' engraved on it. She hugged it to her chest and, through her tears, told Mary, "I will never, ever forget this Christmas, not ever." They both hugged, and we all took a special coffee break; after all, it was Christmas.

Then, Red opened up her wide-brimmed sun hat from me and said, "Even Indians get sunburned, and she especially loved that it was flaming red.

My next present was a heavy red flannel shirt from Mary that fit me perfectly, and the collar label only read Pendleton on one part of the label and Oregon on the other part. It is very wearable, in great shape, and 100 percent wool. It's great for the winters up here.

The following two presents, given to Mary and me, were somewhat identical and both from Red. We opened them together, and they were baby backpacks, one pink and one blue.

Mary said, "Not today, but the day after tomorrow; a short walk was called for if the weather was favorable. Our children live in the 'Wilds of Colorado' now and might as well get used to it sooner than later."

I got a nice flask from Mary since the other one I had was on the mantel and was full of wolf teeth marks. And she looked at the flask on the mantel and said, "Take that, you dead ass wolf."

Red got a pair of those gardening shoes made of rubber from Mary, and I got her a gardening apron with multiple pockets for tools so she didn't have to carry a bucket. She was ecstatic.

In addition to the 30-30 rifle, the clerk threw in an old and well-worn book on the history of the 30-30 for free. He said, "He thought that the gun, the red shirt, and the book were all from the same family and had been part of the store for years when it first was just a thrift shop, which was around the 1920s or so, but he wasn't sure.

The last gifts, again to both Mary and me, were turquoise crosses, which I was sure Red had had for a very long time. I told Red, "The cross would make a perfect complement to the turquoise stone with the gold veins running through it, which you gave me last year."

And with a big smile, she said, "You remembered." I said as I pulled it out of my shirt and showed her, "I never take it off, as a remembrance of our first Christmas. And I think I will get another thin piece of leather and tie a loop for the cross to hang just below the stone, a two-tiered necklace. Then Mary said, "Once you get the thin leather, I would like a piece of it for my cross as well."

Then Red goes, "Well, you both are in luck because I have enough of the thin leather strap from last Christmas to work for both of you." So that was settled, to everyone's satisfaction, especially Red's.

After getting the gun and the stuff that came with it, I couldn't help but wonder: the 1920s? But that would have to wait for another time. All in all, the almost-forgotten Christmas was a complete success, which called for more coffee cake and more special coffee.

Then, even after all that coffee, Mary hit the bed and was sound asleep within minutes. Red and I went out and gave the horses a special treat of sugar cubes and oats, which they really appreciated. The cows, a somewhat recent purchase, got a small salt lick, which goes outside in the near future. If it were left to the cows' prerogative, they would eat it entirely and make themselves sick.

Mary did her evening baby feeding, and then we dove into a dinner of pan-fried elk steak, mashed potatoes with steak gravy, and green beans. With blueberry pie and ice cream for dessert. What a Christmas day it had been. God is good! Oh, and the snifters of the good stuff really topped off the evening.

Before I dropped off, as usual, I lay there and thought about the future, and one thing that really popped out was Idaho, and probably in May. The babes would be around five months or so and should be okay to travel. Frank happened to be a master samurai swordsman, as I was, and I needed to knock off my dust and get some serious training in, just in case. And as I drifted off, I made a mental note to tell Mary the plan and get her ideas on it. And then, I was gone.

The following day, before anyone else was up, I called the coroner. I explained to him that I had gone to high school with Mareilene Johnson and knew her mother.

At this point, I lied, plain and simple. I told him that I had finally tracked her mother to Long Beach, California. I didn't tell her about her daughter, but she was wondering and was so worried that she hadn't shown up in California. She supposedly said, "No calls, no nothing," and then continued and said, "The last time she had talked to Mary, she had said that she was going to go through Cortez, and then north to Interstate 70 west, And then south on Interstate 15. She said she had something to tell her when she got to California, but she said she was going to spend Christmas with friends in St. George, Utah."

Before I broke the news to her, I wanted to know her disposition and the baby's remains. Then the coroner said, "Good thing you called; we keep the deceased for around forty-five days or so and then cremate and bury in the cemetery here."

I said, "Please hold off on all that until I contact her today. Is that okay?"

He said, "No problem. Give me a call after you get in touch, and let me know, okay? If you want, we can cremate the bodies, and you can take the urn to California, especially since they are pretty much cremated already." I said, "I will call you today, but that sounds like a good idea, as bad as it is going to sound to tell it."

He goes, "I feel for you, but just let me know. I can have it done today, and you can pick up the urn this afternoon, no charge, as long as you sign a release."

I said, "Thanks, you have been a great help. God bless!" "You too," he said.

About that time, Red came out of her room, and I asked her to do me a favor. Red said, "No problem, what do you need?" "Two things," I said, "the first, give Margie a call and ask her if she would like a visitor, 'you,' and the second, talk to her about a baby shower." I then said, "I need to talk to Mary about something serious, 'her sister and baby's funeral.

I thought about it this morning and called the coroner. They were going to cremate what was left of the bodies, and I lied and told him I tracked down her mom in California. And that I wanted to know the disposition of the bodies before I talked with her again since I lied and told him I hadn't told her anything, really."

Red said, "I will call right now, and if it is okay, I will take Sly for a walk so you two can talk."

I said, "Thanks, you are a gem. And if we do end up going to California for about a week, can you handle things around her?"

And Red said, "Doing that is a piece of cake, for all you whine about feeding the horses and cows."

Mary came out of the bedroom and said, "The babes are finished feeding, and now I am going to take a shower."

I said, "Sounds like a plan to me. Red is taking Sly for a walk, and I am going to have a special coffee and relax for a bit."

Then Mary said as she closed the bedroom door, "Okay, see you in a bit. I am only going to rinse off; my hair is fine for another day or so."

Red goes, "I am calling as we speak." And she did, and Margie said, "Come on over, sounds like a great idea."

Then Red, with a smile on her face, said, "Since it is so cold out, I think I will need a special coffee to go." And she headed to the bedroom to quickly get dressed. And within a few, I had her coffee ready, and she and Sly were out the door just as Mary came out of the bedroom. Mary said to Red, "See you in a while." As the door shut. And then, since there wasn't an easy way to broach the subject, I said, "Mary, take a seat, and I will get us a couple of shots. We have to talk, okay?"

Mary looked at me and said, "Is there something wrong?"

I said, "Not wrong, just neglected, that's all." And as I can see the worry building up, she says, "Shot and talk, and talk straight out. No beating around the bush, okay?"

I grab two shots, and we both shoot them, and I say, "Your sister and baby's funeral!" She says, "Oh my god, what are we going to do?" "That is what we are going to discuss, my wife.

But let me tell you what I have done so far. I have called the coroner, and they are going to cremate the bodies. And I know this is going to sound horrible. But, I said, it was the only decent way since the fire . . ."

Mary says, "I understand. But I feel sick to my stomach, and I/we haven't done anything before now. What must my mother think? She is probably worried sick. What are we going to do?"

I said, "My thought, and this is based upon something you said at the crash site about California. And really, until this morning, I had forgotten all about it. But I think it will be hard on you and the kids, but news like this should be delivered in person. Let's go to California.

My question is, where in California are we going?"

Mary sat in silence, held up her shot glass, and I proceeded to fill both of them. And she said, "On the California side of Reno, in Truckee. I thought to myself, *Great, I told the coroner, Long Beach. That way, any search would be way off base.* Then I said, "I already asked Red if she could take care of the place for a week or so, and she said no problem. And just so you know, she knows what we are discussing, and she took Sly over to Margie's to discuss a baby shower for you, especially since we are running on a limited amount of clothing for the two of them."

Then she asked, "Will your truck make it there and back?"

I said, "Probably yes, but I have a new, used truck I am going to buy this week, and it is a crew cab, so that baby seats won't be a problem. My question is, do you want to do it this way or fly your Mom into Durango or Farmington and have a service here?

It is your choice. I will go either way, and you know it." Again, she signaled with her glass and said, "We fly her here! She can fly from Reno to Vegas and then to Durango. The kids and I are not up for a trip of that magnitude at this point. I will call her today and have her on the next flight she can get. I will tell her it is 'very' important that I talk to her in person. She knows me well enough that if I say that, no questions will be asked until she is here, and I am ready to sit down and talk. That is with you and Red by my side for support. Deal?"

"Deal," I said, "but I am still going into town today to get the urn and my new used truck, okay."

"Okay," said Mary, and she went on, "I want their ashes buried up by your rock. Is that okay with you?"

I said, "It would be my honor to have her and the baby there, but that will not happen, as I am sure you know, at least until spring." Until then, we can have Fr. John do the funeral at the church and keep the urn here by the fireplace if that is all right with you. I am pretty sure Red . .."

"Red, what?" said Red as she walked in the door.

I said, "You won't mind having the urn, with the ashes of Dareilene and baby, here by the fireplace until spring, when we can place it in the earth up by my rock. Am I right?"

Red says, "That's fine by me. I just recently scattered my husband's ashes in the mountains after having the urn in our home for a while, and with that, the case is settled."

And I see I am behind. "So, Joe, would you be so kind to pour?" As I humbly said, "One coming up, Red, and so you are caught up on everything, Mary is going to call her mother and have her come here as soon as possible for the news. So, we will be having a guest."

"Great!" said Red. "That way, Mom will be here for the baby shower that Margie and I just planned for next Saturday."

Mary, with much trepidation, says, "Let me get this call over with, and then we will discuss the 'baby shower.'" Mary calls her mom and says, "Mom, I need you to get on a plane as soon as possible and fly into either Farmington or Durango; Durango would be best, but whichever you can get here the soonest on.

I have very good news and very bad news, but I have to tell you each piece of news in person! Okay?

Mary's Mom says, "I will call you back probably within the hour and let you know."

Mary says, "Thanks, Mom, I knew you would understand."

Within forty minutes, Mary's mom called and said, "I will be in Durango tomorrow afternoon about four." "We will be there to pick you up. Thanks, Mom, and love you!" said Mary and told the news to me and Red.

I said, "I will call the coroner and pick up the ashes this afternoon, right before I pick up my new used truck. I will call the owner in a few and let him know."

Mary goes, "Red, tomorrow I will feed the kids just before we go, so they should be down for a good four hours. Do you mind watching them?" Red smiles and says, "The World's best stepmom is at your service, my lady. By the way, does Mom have a shot or so occasionally?"

Mary says, "I know she has for years. And considering what I have to tell her, I am sure she will have more than one. In fact, I guarantee it!"

Red says, "Then Joe, pick up four bottles of the good stuff while you are in town. I am sure we need some today, tonight, and definitely tomorrow night." I said, "I think that is a great plan, Red, especially for a woman!"

CHAPTER TWELVE

I took care of the calls to the coroner and the guy selling the truck, and everything was a go. The coroner said, "The ashes and urn would be ready around three." I said, "I would be there shortly after that to pick them up." He said, "See you then."

When I talked to my truck guy, he asked, "What are you going to do with your old truck? Tell you what? I know you use it regularly, so it must be running well, and it looks pretty good. What do you say if I took four thousand off the price of mine, and I'll take yours in trade?"

I thought for a minute *I could probably get six for it, but then I would have to get it back here, clean it up, advertise it, and so on*, so I said, "Deal, I will bring my title."

He said, "Okay, see you around three-thirty." Then, all I had to do was get my stuff out of my truck, put it in the barn, grab my title, and I was ready to go. I should be right on time all the way around. It was already 2:30, so I told the ladies, "I will be back in about three hours or so. Is there anything else they need while I am out?"

Red said, "While you are at the liquor store, grab a couple of bottles of wine, and remember, you are getting the 'good stuff,' right?" I said, "Right, Red. The good stuff it is."

I grabbed my jacket and keys, both sets and headed for my truck. I backed up to the barn and emptied all my stuff, which was really only my essentials, especially my two guns under the seat and my chainsaw. Then, I was on my way, and I honked goodbye to the ladies as I left.

The first stop was the coroner. I walked in, and he handed me the urn and said, "No charge and no paperwork! I just felt so bad that no one had claimed her and her baby . . . well, it just felt good that someone went to the trouble to find her mother. Good luck with telling her the bad news, he said with tears in his eyes as he turned away."

I said, "God bless," with tears in my eyes and the urn under my arm.

My second stop was to get the truck and swap mine out. I said to George, "Well (as I looked at my truck), she has gotten me through a lot of rough spots like you wouldn't believe." And I thought, *even I don't believe it, now that I think about it.*

"But I am looking forward to a newer truck, and the additional seats and doors will make things much more convenient. So, I think this deal works well for both of us."

George said, "I agree. He handed me his signed title, and I handed him mine."

Then he said, "I thought your last name was Everlasting?"

"It was," I said. "But I had it changed years ago to Johnson. Can you imagine having a last name like Everlasting, and my father's name was Peter; think about that for a second. Here, check out my license."

"Yep, that's you and your poor dad," said George, chuckling. We swapped keys, and I drove away. It even had a full tank, just like I left mine for him. I stopped at the Colorado Department of Motor Vehicles, transferred the title, and got a temporary one for the rear window, which I quickly taped to the back window of the truck.

I called my car insurance, transferred my new truck to my policy, and removed my old one. Then, with four bottles of the 'good stuff' and two bottles of wine, I was on my way home in my new four-door, four-by-four truck, which just happened to be red. Red would like that!

By the time I got home, it was around seven, and dinner was just being put on the table as I pulled up. But Red and Mary came out to see our new transportation, and Mary said, "It is perfect. There is room for two car seats with room to spare in the middle."

And Red goes, "I guess, she said, "The middle would be for me?"

And I said, "On the reservation, all the squaws ride in the back!" And boy, did that punch in the gut get my attention. And Mary said, "And you deserve to ride in the back after that comment, and maybe even sleep on the couch!" And I said, "I humbly apologize to my best friend of many years now; please forgive this humble ass." Red goes, "What do you think, Mary?"

"Well," said Mary, "he did sound pretty contrite. Okay, this one time . . ."

We all headed in for dinner, and I felt good about not riding in the back or sleeping on the couch. Open mouth and insert foot, Joe! I thought to myself. *But that shot of the 'good stuff'" mellowed everyone out. Dinner was delicious, with a sort of vegetarian theme. We had corn on the cob, green beans, and mashed potatoes with butter, creamed spinach, and sliced tomatoes.* I said, "Well ladies, I know a lot of this meal was fresh, and the rest was canned, so why the vegetarian, and where did you get the fresh veggies?"

"Mary's idea," said Red. We took the kids for a walk, which they weren't really thrilled about, but they didn't cry. Then, as a turning point, we went to Margie's. She has a greenhouse and more than they can eat, so I answered both questions. "And I thought it was a nice break," said Mary.

And I said, "I loved it. It was a very nice change, very nice indeed." "I really think we should try and do that more often. And I think our digestive tracts will appreciate it as well," I said. And speaking of the digestive tract, I have heard that a bit of whiskey after a meal works wonders as well. Shall I pour?"

Mary goes, "Why yes, kind sir. But I think Red just might have eaten too many sliced tomatoes, and she 'probably' won't partake."

Red said, "I think I had just the 'right' number of tomato slices that a shot would just hit the spot." And everybody laughed as I poured. We savored the shot, and I said, "I think my stomach is saying 'thank you' right now."

Then I said, "Let's get the table cleaned off and the food put away because as much as I don't want to, we have to get on the subject of tomorrow."

"Well, if that is the case," said Red, "we should have another, small one, and then after we are done with the table and stuff, we adjourn to the living room to make a plan. Agreed?"

Mary and I shook our heads and started cleaning up. In a matter of a few minutes, we were all sitting by the fireplace, and I mean all because Dareilene and baby, in spirit, were there with us now, as the urn was at the corner of the fireplace.

With each of us holding a shot, I made a toast: "To Dareilene and . . . Mary, did Dareilene actually have a name picked out?" "Yes, and it was a girl, and she was going to be named . . ." And through a cascade of tears, "Mareilene."

"Okay," I said with us all in tears. "Too, Dareilene and her baby, Mareilene. May God keep them, and we will see them when our jobs on earth are done. Amen!" The shots went down solemnly.

Mary said, "Thanks, Joe. I needed that." I said, "I think we all did."

I got up, grabbed the coffee pot and a cup for each, and said, "Now we plan, and here is what I think we should do. This is a discussion, so please, chime in at any time, 'Got it.'"

Everyone smiled, and I began, "Mary feeds the kids around six, so that means by six-thirty, we can have breakfast, with a special coffee, and relax until eight-thirty or so. Then, after changing, a short walk with the kids, say twenty minutes or so, depending on them, because they will be hungry. And that will have them eating and down by, say, ten. Back up and fed, down by three, and we hit the road for the Durango airport with a half hour to spare. And if worse comes to worst, Mary will have a couple of bottles of milk to warm up, just in case. Okay, your thoughts?"

Mary says, "I think the timing is good, especially the walk thrown in. It gives them something to do besides eat, potty, and sleep. Red, I will milk about a half bottle a piece as a backup, so that should not be an issue. Sounds like a plan to me."

I said, "I will have a shot at, say, eleven to calm my nerves, and then nothing after that until we get home. Mary, you can have one just before we leave to calm yours. And after we pick up your Mom while we are in the car, let's set a ground rule to discuss everything when we get to the house.

I am sure we can discuss why your Mother moved to Truckee, of all places, and go from there. Agreed, Mary?"

Mary said, "Agreed, and in reality, I have been wanting to talk to her about that anyway. It had to do with some man she met about four months ago. She had been alone since my father died of cancer about three years ago. So that should keep us busy."

Then I said, "With that settled, Red, could you be so kind to a fool of a man who stuck his foot in his mouth earlier and pour us one more? I am more than tired after today, and a nightcap would do well to put me to sleep. And tomorrow is going to be a long day, to say the least!"

Red said, "Since you put it so nicely, I will be pleased to oblige the three of us. I think we all need a little nightcap tonight."

She poured, we shot, and all headed for bed, with 'good nights' from all.

CHAPTER THIRTEEN

As we started what was going to be an eventful day, I decided to call Fr. John. As I dialed his number, Mary came out of the bedroom and asked, "Who was I calling?" I replied, "Fr. John, I thought it might be beneficial to have him here when we get back from the airport with your mother. What do you think?"

Mary thought as she got herself a cup of coffee, just plain, and then said, "Joe, I am not sure, but if you think it is a good idea, go for it. She is Catholic, after all, and having a priest here definitely wouldn't hurt. I say yes, give him a call and see if he is available."

And I dialed the last number, and after two rings, "This is Fr. John, how may I help you?" I said, "Fr. John, this is Joe, and I was wondering if you are free tonight to come by?"

Fr. John asks, "Is there anything wrong?"

I said, "Well, we are picking up Mary's mom at the airport. She knows nothing about anything, and on top of that, I picked up Dareilene and the baby's ashes yesterday, so your presence just might be needed."

Fr. John says, "What time do you want me there?"

"We will pick her up around 4:00 PM, and with luggage and all, around 5:30 at the latest," I said.

Fr. John said, "I will be there just a little early, just in case, okay?"
"That sounds fine. See you when we get home," I said.

"Well, that's taken care of. Is there anything else you can think of that we forgot last night?" I asked Mary.

Mary said, "No, not that I can think of unless you can make that clock go faster." "No luck, already tried," said Red, coming out of her room. And she heads for the coffee pot and pours a cup. And I made it strong for a reason, and as she tasted it, she knew the reason and reached into the cupboard and motioned to me and Mary. We both shook our heads yes. Then, we all sat down by the fireplace to warm up twice.

Red goes, "Good call on Fr. John, Joe. We should have thought of that last night."

"Well," I said, "I do my best thinking first thing in the morning with a good strong cup of coffee, straight and quiet, AKA no one else up."

Mary pipes in, "I agree, best thinking time." And then we just sat and wondered what the day would bring. It could be one for the Journal of Life. Especially since tomorrow, I have a feeling there will be a lot to enter." Red goes, "I will grab the book, nature calls."

"Red," I say, "what time is it? I have my cutoff time, and it is Friday; on top of everything else, Highway Patrol will be out in mass all this week between Christmas and New Year's."

Red says, "It's nine, so you have some time yet. Two and breakfast, you should be good to go with no problem."

"Tell you what," I said. "Have two shots waiting in our bedroom when we get home, if you would be so kind. I have a feeling that we will both want one when we get back and going straight to the cabinet might seem a little much. Do you know what I mean?" "I do. And they will be waiting for you when you go in to 'get more comfortable.'"

Well, the rest of the day went like clockwork. The kids even seemed to enjoy the walk. It was a good thing that Mary had got the half bottles ready earlier because they ate like little piglets when we got back. Three o'clock rolled around actually faster than anticipated, and we were out the door and headed for Durango airport right on time. Mary had one last 'good one' before we left. "Just for courage," she said.

And I was right about the highway patrol. As we went by, they already had DUI stops in place or were in the process of setting them up. We arrived at the airport at ten to four, and her Mom's plane was pulling up as we did. We met her at the gate as she got off the plane, where Mary introduced her mother as Hellene and then introduced me as Joe, her husband.

There were no questions from Hellene; she only raised eyebrows, and we went to get her luggage. She had three bags, which made me wonder, how long was she going to stay? But we had plenty of room, so it really didn't make a difference one way or another. I carried two suitcases, and Hellene insisted that she carry the other one. We got into the truck, and the conversation began. "Mary, not to pry, but since I am here now, I can, at least on some things, ask questions, right?" said Hellene.

"Mother," said Mary, "I will just tell you later when we get to our house that we will discuss a questionable topic. Agreed?"

"Agreed," said Hellene. "Okay, let's start with the easy questions first. So I see you have a ring on your finger. How long have you and Joe been married?"

"Mother!" said Mary. You said easy questions first, but if you must know, we got married on December 1st of this year." "Okay, Joe, or is it Joseph?" Hellene asked.

And I answered, "It is Joseph. I had very religious parents who died in a head-on wreck with a drunk driver between Durango and Farmington. And I go by Joe unless Mary is upset with me. And just so you know, I love your daughter more than life itself. And it just so happens that I knew Mary in high school," I said.

Mary started to say something. . . and I said, "Told you so." Straight ahead was a DUI stop. The troopers were pulling over every car coming out of Durango since it was time for people to head home, and a few might stop to have a brew or two on a Friday getting off work.

When it came to my turn in line to show my ID, I was asked to step out of the car. I did as asked but also asked, "Why?" The trooper said, "We are asking all drivers to step out, just as a holiday policy this week. *Strange*, I thought to myself; *I didn't see anyone else getting out of their vehicles.* "Can I see your license and proof of insurance?"

"Officer," I said, "I just bought the truck yesterday, and I called and changed my policy the same day, so I don't have a card, but I have my insurance card if you want to see that." They insure only military personnel or their families. "Oh, that one," said the officer. "There's no need to see it, and you either are or were military serviced by your insurance company. Nam, I take it?" asked the officer.

I said, "Yes, sir, behind enemy lines stuff, but that is all I can say."

"I can tell you haven't been drinking. Do you have any guns in your truck?"

I said, "Yes sir, two 9mms."

And he questioned, "Why two?"

I said, "In case I run out of ammo in the first one, sir." "On your way, soldier, and why did you call me sir?" he asked.

I said, "I could just tell by the way you held yourself that you were an officer. I knew good and bad ones in the bush. I luckily had a great one, and I have a feeling you were a good one as well since you are alive and all."

He shined his flashlight into the car, focused on Mary, and said, "Looks like you have your work cut out for you tonight, sergeant. The sooner you get to it, the better."

"Sir," I said, "just a quick question. Why did I have to get out of my vehicle and most others didn't? "Well, to tell the truth of the matter, your truck matches one used in a bank robbery in Colorado Springs yesterday, and you match the description of the suspect.

And do you really think I would be out here freezing my ass off at a DUI stop if it wasn't for something like that? And that you had a wife and her mother in the car didn't hurt either."

I said, "No, sir, I don't. Good luck, and I hope you catch the asshole and can go home. God bless and be safe!"

As I got into the car, Mary asked, "Why did you say, 'Since you are alive and all,' to that officer?"

I said, "Long story short . . . In the bush in Nam, if you were a bad officer and got your troops killed because of your poor decisions, no more needs to be said."

As I drove away, I thought, *Something was just not right. You know when you get that feeling, and you get it, trust it. Keep your eyes peeled, Joe; something truly isn't right.*

Hellene said, "Mary, it looks like you got yourself an honorable man, to say the least."

"Mother," Mary said, "you don't know the tenth of it and 'later.'" The trip was pretty quiet after that, with the typical questions about how her flights went, and before you knew it, we were pulling into the yard. I grabbed all of the suitcases.

One of the suitcases, the one the Hellene insisted on carrying, rattled like metal on metal. The alarms were going off again, I thought.

Mary took her mother into the house, and Red opened the door as they approached. And she said, "You must be Hellene, my name is Red, and to make it short and sweet, Joe picked me up in a blizzard hitchhiking to Cortez about a couple of years ago now; I had just lost my husband of thirty years, he put me up in his guest room, and for just over two Christmas's we have been close friends and confidants. I cook and clean. He works and provides food and friendship, as well as a shoulder to cry on when I need it. Your daughter couldn't have a better husband and father . . ."

Mary goes, "We haven't gotten there yet, but since we are, Mother, would you like to see your grandchildren?"

Hellene goes, "I knew you had been pregnant, but twins?" But Mary says, "Before that, I need to introduce you to our other guest, Fr. John, who, as they call him, is our Renegade Catholic. Fr. John, my mother, Hellene."

Fr. John says, "Nice to meet you, Hellene."

Hellene says, "Fr. John, wouldn't you be here to offer your wisdom on the many issues at hand?"

Fr. John says, "That is my job, if needed. And may I offer a shot of some very 'good' whiskey before we get started? I think it just might be, as well as a few more, warranted as the evening progresses."

Then I said, "Father, Mary, and I will be getting a bit more comfortable, and we will be right out." We went to our bedroom, shed our coats, downed our shots, kissed, hugged, and said, "God be with us!" And we opened the door to the living room as the shots went down in the kitchen. Then Hellene and Fr. John came into our bedroom, and I thought, *Let the night begin.*

Hellene just stood there and smiled and cried at the same time because she knew there should be three babies and two daughters, but that was yet to come, and she knew it. The shot had taken the sudden chill off, but it was back in spades, and she said, "Mary and Joe, they are beautiful, and there is something 'very' special about them, which I am sure we will be getting to tonight, for sure."

But the smile died, and she said, "I want the bad news about Dareilene and her baby first, as I am sure that is why the Father is here, so let's go sit down, and Father, if you would pour me another, I would greatly appreciate it, because I am sure I am going to need it."

She went and sat by the fireplace, and she couldn't help but notice the urn by the corner, and she cried like a baby. As she sat there and sobbed, we all knew she needed some time of her own with her daughter and unborn child.

We all had a couple of shots, and after ten or so minutes, I quietly said, "I will do the main talking, with everyone chiming in as they see fit. I know the most, so I feel that I can include all the important facts and leave out the ones that don't need to be told, if ever. Agreed."

No one spoke, but they shook their heads in agreement. I grabbed another shot and took three boxes of tissues over to the chairs. I handed Hellene one more shot and a box of tissues, for which she whispered, "Thank you." And I began.

I started with the snowstorm and their car crashing into the guardrail. Mary escaped with a severe head injury, and Dareilene and the baby died instantly in the crash. Then, the fire caused the ice to melt, and the car went off the edge into the canyon.

And then, the most essential part of all. The part that set everything in motion from there on. I told Hellene that Mary said "That God had sent me to save her and her baby (since she thought she only had one baby) from the devil himself who was after her and her baby to kill them because God sent him into this world to be the savior. I said that she threw all her belongings into the car, took Dareilene's out, and threw them into my truck as the car plunged over the edge of the cliff.

Then, Mary, going into shock from her head wound, said, 'Drive like the Devil is on your tail because he is.' The snow was coming down so heavily that our tracks were covered in minutes. In the truck, Mary convinced me, again, that she was telling me the truth about the Devil.

And on top of all that, God had sent me to be their savior from the Devil himself. At Mary's demand, I drove like the Devil was on my tail and made it to the house just as Mary passed out, the worst time for a person in shock.

As I pulled up, I yelled for Red to call Doc and get him over even if he had to come by dog sled. He made it in record time. He stitched her up since that was all he could do in this weather and this far from a hospital. If it could get any stranger, and believe me, it can and does.

Doc walks out and says, "She is in severe shock, and there is really nothing I can do but wait and watch. At this time, I take a shot break, and everyone does the same. Having to relive the night again."

Then Doc goes, "First, she is pregnant with two babies, and to make it even more interesting, she has a fully intact hymen. Second, she has an aura around her that I have never felt before. Even dogs feel it. They are guarding the babies, with Mary a close second."

Then, there is more; as we sit there waiting to see if she and her babies are going to live or die, she speaks softly but loud enough for all in the house to hear.

She says, "God trusts you, Joseph, with his son, and now I know he also trusts you with his daughter. Joseph, you and I are going to be married, and our children will be named Christian Peter Everlasting, Christ Everlasting later, and Hope Mary Everlasting, Hope Everlasting later as well."

At this point, Doc went in, and as he came out, he said, 'She is now resting peacefully, her color is back to normal, and I think she will be just fine. But he goes on, how a woman that was in severe shock only a short while ago, as we all know, and had a severe head laceration is now resting peacefully, I can only say, God only knows, and that I really indeed mean.

Hellene goes, "That is all I can really bear to hear tonight. During the light of day tomorrow, I am sure, will be more appropriate for more telling of this story. Joe, I am sure you left out some of the more gruesome points, and I am sure glad you did. Thanks! I am going to have one more of the 'good' stuff and go to bed. It has already been a long day, and this just made it longer. I know more than I ever wanted to know, and I am sure there is just as much if not much, more to the story that I need to know, but not right now.

I would appreciate it if you all joined me in saluting my other daughter and baby, Joe and Mary, Doc, and everyone, including Fr. John, who I am sure played more of a part in all this than just being here for me tonight.

And then I said, "And most of all to our God, who most say works in mysterious ways. If they only knew what that really meant." We all raised our glasses. "To God, may his power be everlasting, as well as his knowledge! Amen!"

"Amen, was echoed by all, except Hellene, who was crying loudly and went to her room crying, which we were all, 'except me,' sure she would be doing most of the night."

In her bedroom, she pretended to be still crying, but an 'Evil' smile was on her face, as she thought. *They bought all of it: the grieving mother, the tears of grief, and the mental disguise! Mary actually thought her mother's name was Hellene. I had to bite my tongue to keep from laughing.*

The minions who did the background work on this should be commended. Damn, I must be tired; it is I who will be praised. Let those peons rot in Hell. Wait, they are, as she again smiled through her even louder sobs. I am surprised that I didn't kill all of them then and there and be done with it! Especially the priest! Just being in the same room was so vile. But that damn Joe was a wild card I didn't expect, and he would bear watching like a hawk!

But besides Joe, three things stopped me, damn it. First, I need the savior to die of a ritual killing. And secondly, and most importantly, I want the savior's blood, every single drop of it. Oh, the thought of it sliding down my throat.

Thirdly, now I have to get the news out to the emergency line tonight while everyone is asleep! So the Prince will know it is 'I, Hellene' who found the missing savior he was so concerned about. I know I will move up in His Majesty's eyes after this! And the 'Evil' smile emerged again. Along with the fake sobbing, she added a wail to ensure a 'sympathy' effect.

After everyone had gone to bed and was asleep except me, I got up and unplugged the phone line from the jack, and if you didn't know that it was behind the fireplace, you would never know that it had been unplugged. I pushed the chair back in front of the cord, just in case. I got back up quietly around two, on the pretense to make sure that I had locked the front door. And wouldn't you know it, there was Hellene, with the phone in her hand, and she said quietly, as not to wake anyone else, "I remembered that I was going to call my sister and let her know I made it, but as I picked up the phone, I figured it was too late, and that I would call her in the morning. Hope I didn't wake you?"

I said, "I woke up thinking, '*Did I lock the front door?*' With all the whiskey and just everything else, I wanted to make sure the front door was locked. We are out in the sticks, but you still have to be careful."

Of course, I had locked it. But I continued my story, "Besides, I saw the phone guys working on the lines just before we turned off the highway. We have had some strong storms lately, so the lines are probably down anyway."

And I thought, *As if she already didn't know!*

I went back to the bedroom, and even though I slept, I slept 'lite.' You learn that in Nam, or if you don't know, you don't leave Nam. And since I wasn't really sleeping, I got up around four-thirty. First of all, I hadn't asked Red if she had gotten to the animals, and if not, they were going to be hungry, and after last night, I couldn't really sleep.

I kissed Mary, and she said a sleepy "Morning" and was back to sleep, really before she even woke up. I dressed quietly, grabbed my jacket, and headed out to the barn. And yes, they had been fed, but they never turned down food, ever. I lit a fire and let it burn for a while since it was just getting to daylight, and it was always the coldest part of the morning. That is because as the peaks catch the light of the sun, the colder air comes cascading down the mountains into the valleys.

Then, after a little while, after the fire burned down, I banked it back and headed back in. I wanted it warm to show Hellene our work on the wind spinners, as a needed break in the day, and to keep 'everyone' busy.

As I walked in, I smelled coffee and looked to see who was up. It was Hellene with a small fire and a cup of coffee, which I could smell as 'special' coffee. She did the hush symbol with her finger, and I quietly went to the kitchen for my cup of 'special' coffee, especially since today would probably be tense not only with all the talking but with what else had transpired coming home last night, as well as what went on in the middle of the night.

With coffee poured, I put another log on the fire and asked Hellene, "Is it all right if I sit down on the couch with her?" She shook her head yes and went back to her coffee. I sipped mine for a short while, and then I heard Mary call out, "Mother, please help me put the babies down. I can do it myself, but it is much easier with someone to help."

I said, "I guess we weren't as quiet as we thought we were." Hellene just stood up and went into the bedroom. She took Christian, holding him with his blanket wrapped around him, as Mary handed him to her. She stood up and put Hope in her bed. She covered both of them up, and they were sound asleep in seconds.

Hellene said, "Mary, go out and get yourself a coffee, and I will be out in a few. I need a little time with my grandchildren if you don't mind?" Mary said, "Mother, please take all the time you need. We aren't going anywhere." And then she left Hellene with the children and shut the door behind her.

After Mary left, Hellene tried to put her hands on each child, but the burning was too much for one of her kind to touch anyone who was still of 'God.' She just shrugged it off and silently thanked the 'Prince' for this stroke of good luck. And to think, he, Christian, could be the savior they thought had died in the car crash. She cursed to herself that the phone lines were down and that she couldn't tell anyone the 'great' news.

And those damn dogs are going to have to die as well. They growl every time I come near these children. I swear, I am going to enjoy all of this killing by myself. Oh, the joy of it all, as she stood there listening to them breathe, thinking how soon those would be their last breaths, and she smiled her 'evil' smile again and headed out to the living room.

While all that was taking place in the bedroom, as Mary left the room, I joined her and poured a shot for each of us. They went down quickly, and then I poured an additional shot in each of the two coffee cups, added coffee, and pointed Mary toward the couch by the fireplace, where we sat side by side. Mary looked at me with a 'what's up' look in her eyes. I said very quietly, "Mary, I know you trust me, but deep down in your heart, do you really trust me?"

"Joe," Mary said. "You are scaring me, and you know I trust you with everything I hold dear in my life, including my life itself. What is wrong?"

Thinking to myself, I said, "What I am going to tell you, you will have to believe me, like no other time. Just listen to what I am going to say and know I wouldn't be saying it if I didn't believe it to be God's truth!" Mary looked deep into my eyes and said, "No matter what you say, I will believe. I would believe you if you said my mother was the Devil himself if you said it right now."

"Mary," I said, " not the Devil himself, but one of his minions." She looked at me, and she knew I wasn't kidding.

And then she whispered, with tears in her eyes, "But she is in the room, alone with my babies." I grabbed her and held her tight and close and said, "The dogs are there, and I have been watching them since she got here, and they don't 'trust' her one iota. They are safe. But you are going to have to let me handle this my way. Because it has to be done just right to make sure no others get any information. Got it?"

I also said, "I already unplugged the phone earlier last night, which was a good thing. Because I caught her trying to use it after everyone, except me, was asleep. I told her I saw the phone guys working on the lines as we were coming home, so the lines were probably down anyway. Which I am sure she knew already. And the coughing fit during the 'Amen' of the last toast. And last but not least, as I moved that third suitcase 'she' insisted upon carrying herself, it had a metal-on-metal rattle inside. All of which set off alarms in my head, and I am sure I am right."

"Mary, I said, "I am so sorry, but I am afraid your mother is probably dead, and this thing, or better said, a minion, and if I am right, a very powerful minion, has taken her place. And after saying that, my love, you are going to have to play the most important part of your life for you, your babies, and the rest of us. I know for them, you would rip her throat out in a heartbeat, but leave that to me. It, like I have said, has to be done and done right."

Mary looks at me with a face etched with fear, and a mother's determination to protect her children says, "Got it!"

And I say, "Good, and no one else knows, not even Red unless I decide to tell her because I need her.

I am a grown man, and I know how to kill and how to kill efficiently! Let me do what I have been trained to do, and everything will work out.

Now, sit back, enjoy your coffee, and 'know' her death will be slow and painful, I promise. Your 'mom' will be back out soon, and I am sure she would love for you to tell her about . . ."

"About what," said Hellene as she came out of the bedroom, just beaming."

"About Thanksgiving, the wedding, and the Christmas births, just to name a few," said Mary. Hellene thinks to herself; *they believe it all, the scum they are* as she says, "They were born on Christmas? Well, I would never have guessed."

And then Mary, cool, calm, and collected, took over the storytelling, thank 'God.'

I got myself another 'good shot' and brought two others for the ladies and just sat and listened. I listened and thought about how *to dispose of her minion body. I knew I could kill her, slowly and painfully, as I said, but I had to make it look like she never even got here. I was working on a plan that had not yet been formed in my mind, but it would be soon, very soon. Hellene will know what and who kills her, when and as it happens, but nobody else will, with the exception of Mary and Red.*

Red walked out of her bedroom yawning and asked, "Did I miss anything? After last night, I slept like a baby." I said, "Not much; the ladies will fill you in later. Would you care for a coffee or a 'special coffee'?"

Red rolls her eyes, like only she can, and says, "Only a 'man' would ask a stupid question like that?"

CHAPTER FOURTEEN

"**M**other," said Mary, "since we have been doing all of the talking, I would like to know what has been going on in your life for, say, the last year or so since we have not had more than just chit-chat on the phone. And how in the heck did you end up in Truckee, California, of all places?"

"Well, do you want the good news or the bad news first?" Asked Hellene.

Mary and Red look at each other, and Red says, "Tell you what, for a change, Joe is going to pick. He does this to us all the time, and I do mean all the time. Right, Mary?" "Right, you are, Red."

Then, looking over at Joe, Mary asked, "What will it be, Joe? The good news or the bad news? Or, as you often do, both? They are either both good or, more often than not, both bad." So, I answered, "The 'good' first."

Hellene says, "Okay, the 'good' first. Well, I made it here in one piece; I still have some money in the bank, about 15,000 dollars, my health is good, and I am no longer married. That is about it for the 'good' news."

Mary swallows and asks, "Ah, when did you get married? And I thought you had a pretty good nest egg from Dad? Also, if I remember correctly, you had a house. It had a mortgage, but it was a house in a good location.

Mary looks bewildered, and I say, "I guess it is time for the 'bad' news, right, Hellene?"

"Joe, have people ever said you have a way with words?" said Hellene.

"Mother!" Mary harshly yet restrainedly said, "Okay, I was waiting for more good news, but apparently, there isn't any. And while I am at it, what happened to all of Dad's stock investments, the ones that he always kept in reserve? 'They,' he always said, 'would be redeemed only in dire circumstances?'" Mary got up and walked to the bedroom to check on the kids.

Hellene was caught totally off guard and called out to Mary. She stopped and turned with her arms crossed, and she continued quickly, "Well, I am sure you have heard the saying 'Love is blind.' Well, in my case, it was deaf and dumb as well. I married a man named Mark Montague, whom I 'thought' had money, but it turned out it was someone else's money. Mark was a con artist, a swindler, and, on top of that, a gambler, a lousy gambler at best.

To make matters even worse, he had two 'other wives' besides me. At least I was able to get divorced, but not until I basically lost everything. If I hadn't made a loan to your aunt Joan a while back, and she was paying me back into an account that Mark didn't know about, I wouldn't even have the 15,000 dollars.

And he disappeared like he never was. Leaving me penniless in an apartment in someone else's name; the rent was four months in arrears. The apartment manager tried to have me evicted. I said No, and he called the police, who were going to arrest me, but I sobbed and whimpered, 'I was just sleeping with him, and they let me go.

I calmly replied, "They just let you go as simple as that? That doesn't sound like any police that I know of. Didn't they at least do a background check on you?"

Hellene said, "No, but they did do one on Mark and found out he was a felon wanted in several states. I figured that is why they believed my story."

I thought, *Believed your story, my ass. They would have held you for at least twenty-four hours and checked out your story as well: another checkmark against you.*

Hellene thought, *even more intelligent than I gave him credit for.*

As I said, "Wow, I have heard bad news before, but that, to say the least, tops a lot."

Mary, barely controlling her tone, asks, "Mom, what are you going to do?"

And before Hellene could answer, I said, "Well, for one thing, I guess you will be staying here until, well, until we can think of something. The guest room is yours as long as you need it."

And then Mary kicks in, "Yes, Joe is right, I think from what you say, at the present, we are it, at least for the winter. Any issues, Red?" Red goes, "How do you think I ended up here?"

Thinking fast, I say, "I think 'news' like that deserves a shot. And a big one at that, wouldn't you say, Mary?"

"Yes, Joe. And as you always say, at least a big one, maybe two," said Mary.

Mary walked over and hugged her mom, who was crying like a baby and said, "Mom, as Joe's mom always said to him, 'if you need something bad enough, God will provide. And that is why we are here for you."

"Now, Joe, start providing those shots. I think they are well in order about now," said Red. I'm on it, Mistress Red!" I spoke. As I was pouring, I thought, *I was sure glad Dad had me hooked on that 25 percent savings plan! We were going to need it, if for nothing more than somehow eliminating Hellene without a single, solitary trace. And that plan was almost to fruition.*

Well, with that crisis now out in the open, everyone, especially Hellene, seemed to relax and enjoy the day. Mary told her mom all about Thanksgiving and Fr. John, about the wedding blizzard, and finally, about the birthing of the twins. She left out the wolves for me at another time. Another extraordinary time.

But then I had an idea. Well, it was an idea I had already planned, but no one else knew, so here goes: "Hellene, would you really like to see something special? I mean, something you don't see every day?"

"Why yes," said Hellene. Red and Mary thought I had a few too many until I told everyone to grab their coats, and Mary wrapped the kids up in a couple of blankets to go to the barn.

With the kids wrapped up like cocoons and us in our jackets, we headed for the barn. I let everyone in and then turned on the light, and all the spinners came to life.

Hellene says, "Where did all these come from?" Mary proudly says as she bites her tongue, "Mom, the three of us made them to 'kill' time (she looked directly at me) while waiting for me to give birth. They are called 'Wind Spinners.' To make them, we went to all the neighbors and collected everything from coconut shells to wooden Dutch shoes and chalices: anything that would catch the wind. What do you think?"

With awe in her eyes, she walked by and spun each one. (That is except the one with the Bible and the chalices on it. I wonder why?) I was literally amazed that we made treasures from junk. She said, "How long did this take you?"

Red says, " It took two very long weeks, but in the end, it was worth it. And Joe, we still need to deliver these to the owners, probably this week."

And I say, "Well, we do have a new babysitter if she is willing?"

"Yes," said Hellene (way too excitedly for me and Mary). Then I said, "That way, all the builders can deliver and get credit for all their hard work. And if I remember right, there is a 'baby shower' at the house on Saturday, so we will have to have them out of here before then because I will have a pony keg out here for the guys while the ladies party inside. Sounds like a plan to me. What do you think, Red?"

"I think," says Red, "for a 'man,' you still never cease to amaze me. And it is cold out here. Inside all, babies first." Mary said, "Red, I thought 'we' were going to be discussing the baby shower first?" Red said, "I think we just did." As I closed the barn up, Red said, "Thanks for saving my tail there."

"No problem," I said. "What else are men good for besides saving women's tails? And coming out in the cold is a damn good reason to 'warm' up with a shot when we get back in, wouldn't you think so?"

Red says, "Damn, you are on a roll!"

And I thought to myself, *Red, you wouldn't believe how much of a' roll' I am on at the moment. You really wouldn't, but you will tomorrow.*

As we get inside, I look at Mary, wink, and loudly say, "Mary, before you take your coat off, put the kids in bed in the bedroom with the dogs and leave the bedroom door open so Red can hear them if one of them cries. I want your opinion on where we might build a 'mother-in-law' house on the east or west side of the building."

Mary says, "Okay, Joe, just give me a second to put the babies down. They're tired anyway and should sleep soundly for at least a couple of more hours, and it shouldn't take us too long, should it?"

"No, not long at all. Basically, one walk around the house should do it. I'll wait outside. See you in just a few," I said.

Mary comes out, grabs my arm, and almost silently screams, "This had better be worth it."

"It is," I said. "And I have my 9mm with me, Red in the house, and the 'dogs,' need I say more. And we will spend the majority of the time we are out here on the north side, which happens to have our bedroom in it.

Okay?"

"Yes," said Mary, somewhat angry and nervous at the same time. "What is your plan? I take it that is why we are out here, right?"

"Yes, it is," I said. Now listen, and don't talk. We only have a short time, and I have a lot to say, much of which you will 'object' to, but you said you trusted me, and I trust that you do."

"Joe," said Mary, "I am not sure if I like the fact that I am going to 'object' to most of what you are going to say, but, and this is very important, I trust you like no other besides God himself. Got it!" I just shook my head yes.

And I continue, "Now, first of all, since she is the only one here who can make a 'sacrifice,' which is required to kill a savior, it will take time. And in my plan, she has to do it all in silence, including the dogs, so again, time is in my favor."

Mary couldn't resist, "Okay, mister minion killer, what is your plan? And why are you concerned about how 'long' everything will take her?"

"It is because we are going to leave her alone," I said quietly. Mary's eyes were tearing, her mouth was moving, and finally, she very quietly and calmly said, "What in God's fucking name, forgive me, are you; No, why am I even going to consider it?"

"There are two reasons. First, she has to trust that she has time to take care of the dogs without firing a shot. She will have to lure them into another room with a steak or something similar so she can access the babies.

Then, she has to prepare the 'sacrificial' table in the barn with a pentagram and bless it. Then, she has to get the babies and bind them, say the required chants, and then you get the rest. "And all this time, I take it we will be delivering 'wind spinners,' right?" said Mary.

"Yes and no. Yes, you and Red will be delivering the spinners, while, as soon as we make the bend up the road, I will get out of the truck and quickly backtrack to the house to do what I do best: KILL!"

But like I said before, "It has to be done right, and at just the right time, in the process. Remember I told you I was a genius? I lied; I scored twenty-five points above that level. And just to let you know, I know my 'Dark Arts.' I know them better than most scholars because I have seen them in operation in foreign lands! I know. I wish I didn't, but I do."

"So, I think we have decided on the southwest corner of the property by the old oak. Agreed?" Said loud enough to be heard in the house. Mary bucked up and smiled, and through gritted teeth, "I agree, but I am going to. . ."

"Nothing, nothing at all except to know she will have suffered 'greatly.' You have my word and God's word on that as well. Shall we go in and make the announcement?"

"We shall, my love, we shall. And I shall have a smile on my face, knowing what tomorrow will bring all night long."

Then I took Mary's hand, and we walked back into the house. "Well, it took a little longer than we thought it would, but Mary will announce the choice. Drum roll!" I spoke. Mary smiles sweetly and says,

"Red you know that old oak on the southwest corner of the cleared property? That is the place. Close enough to the main house, with plenty of privacy, when needed. Good drainage, and the view is to 'die' for! If I say so myself, mother. If you would like, I can take you out there right now, and you can see it."

Hellene, staying in character, says, "Yes, and Red, would you like to join the women and leave the 'man' to babysit? "Okay, fine, but if there isn't any whiskey left, it wasn't me," I quipped.

Red follows with, "Well, we had better take our own to toast the new diggings come spring. Ladies, do you agree?"

Mary goes into her best southern accent and says, "Why, Red, I do believe you have come up with a truly, almost 'manly' solution for the whole dilemma facing us damsels in distress."

And I say, "Your humble servant eagerly awaits your return, with bated breath, or should I more correctly say, whiskey breath."

When the ladies return, I will look like I have had several shots because most of the whiskey in my bottle was poured into a different bottle for another time. Plus, my wits were needed for the next twenty-four hours or so.

But as I heard them approaching the house, I poured two shots for two reasons. The first reason and shot were because I wanted one. The second reason and shot were primarily for our 'temporary visitor. Its purpose was for Hellene to think I was well on my way to being drunk.

As the ladies came back in, everyone was laughing, including Mary. That was unless you looked closely at her eyes. Then all you saw was hate! Unmitigated hate that only the death of Hellene could take away.

I thought to myself, *What does a person, if she is a person, get for a last meal on death row?*

"Red," I asked, "what are Hellene's choices for dinner?"

Red says, "In about an hour, I can make up just about anything. How about creamed green beans over mashed potatoes paired with thinly sliced elk back strap, still rare, with wild onions and just seasoned with salt and a touch of curry? And a side of summer squash with brown sugar and cinnamon?

And if you can handle a processed crust, we can finish with a cherry pie and pecan ice cream. Everyone cheered, especially Hellene, who thought this was a meal created just for her to celebrate, but in her mind, Hellene was celebrating the taste of blood, fresh from a baby, a savior's throat, but she could wait, but only for a few more hours.

The meal was really to die for and not in the way one would think. It was excellent, and who would have thought that cherry pie and pecan ice cream together would be utterly delightful? I made sure, without being overly so, that Hellene's glass always had some in it, never full, just enough to warrant another little bit, quite often.

Totally stuffed, I said to Red, "Now I know why I picked you up on the highway that night. You are a master cook! And I do not say that lightly since I have eaten at many a five-star restaurant that couldn't have rivaled that meal."

Later, I rechecked the phone and said, "Still dead. They must be replacing a main line. You would think they would have the courtesy to let you know." Hellene seemed pleased that it didn't work. She said, "Sometimes, it is good to be cut off from those that want stuff from you all the time." And she chuckled to herself as if it was an insider joke. I thought, '*He who laughs last . . .*'

Well, it was getting late, and I said, "I think I will hit the hay. While you three were surveying the southwest forty, I was surveying a twenty-year-old Johnny Walker, and I think he stomped on me while I was surveying. Mary, are you ready?"

"Yes, my fine, sir. I am ready for all the deliverables for tomorrow, and I hope they all appreciate the thought put into them. Good night, and May God bless us one and all."

As we walked into the bedroom, Mary looked at me and said quietly, "You are confident that your plan will work? I know I shouldn't even ask, but the mother in me is screaming, and screaming, run! Run as fast and as far away with your babies as you can. I am sorry, but just tell me again that you have it under control and are confident it will

KILL her slowly and painfully. You promise me that right now, and I will sleep with angels." I said, "I promise! Now, do you remember where you put that cross that I found when I was building this place?" I asked her.

Mary thought for a moment, and she said, "I think it is. Yes, I know it is on the outside front wall above the door, just hanging by a nail. It's not nailed in, just hanging there. Why?"

I said, "You wanted it painful and slow, right, and I want her to be without marks; that is why I want it."

"You will drop me off, and under no circumstances are you to come back here until I call you at Margie's! Do you understand? I will take care of the rest. And the devil will have one less minion to do his bidding because there will not be a single trace of her on this earth when I am finished. So Help Me God. Now, my fine wife, get into bed; I have a surprise for you."

"A surprise? Now? What?" said Mary as she literally jumped into bed. I got in beside her and pulled her close to me. I kissed her lips, her chin, and her neck, and I reached my goal as I kissed her nipple. I sucked gently, then harder, and only heard a "moan, and oh, Joe, you shouldn't, but please don't stop."

And I wasn't, as my hand worked its way between her legs, and she shivered, and again, she said, "Please don't stop." as she handed me her other breast. Within minutes, she came hard and long, and once was not enough! And then she found me, and the rest was history. Let's say, even though I slept light, just in case, Mary was gone with the angels while wrapped in my arms. And I was the happiest man on earth, with Hell coming tomorrow.

Tomorrow rolled around, and as usual, it started with the chores of the horses, cows, and dogs. Then, a fire warms up the barn, and back into the house for coffee and quiet time in front of the fire.

As I sat and enjoyed my coffee, I was planning my day. I was primarily planning for every possible 'tangent' that could throw a monkey wrench in my plans and how I would deal with it.

There were a lot of things that could go awry, and I knew it. I had already taken my samurai sword and the cross from over the door out to the barn. Again, that assumption of her using the barn could be totally wrong. But my gut said it would happen there, so that is where I planned to execute my plan and Hellene.

As I had just finished my first coffee, the guest room door opened and out came a smiling Hellene dressed to kill, and I do not say that lightly. She wore a shiny red blouse with a high collar, buttoned up to the top, a black leather vest, black jeans, and high-top boots. I said, "You look pretty good today; what is the occasion?"

She said, "Oh, this old outfit. My ex loved me in it, and it fits so well and is comfortable, so I thought, why not? Besides, it is my birthday, didn't you know?"

"No," I said, "I had no clue. Happy birthday. And I thought, *what a great day to die as well. And it hit me, for a woman as, let me say, as well endowed as Hellene, she always wore a blouse or top, buttoned high, as if to conceal something, not to be seen. And I smiled and wondered, what was hidden in that cleavage? I said*, "I am getting a 'special coffee,' and it is your birthday. Would you like one?"

"Why, thank you. That is sweet and thoughtful. Thinking, *for someone who is going to die a painful death at my hands today,* I really deserve one. In fact, make it a double, if you would please."

I said, "Believe me, my pleasure." So, being the gentleman I am, I got the 'woman' for nothing but just a term to use her double 'special' coffee. In fact, I made it even more robust, closer to almost a triple, but not quite. I delivered her coffee and started to sit down. But as I did, I said,

"I had better check on Mary and the babies. We have a busy day today, and I hope we can get all the deliveries in between feedings, which are about four hours apart." I went in and closed the door as Mary was feeding the children, which Hellene figured would be their last meal, and asked, "How did you sleep?" Mary said, "Like a dream until I woke up to 'Hell on Earth.'"

I asked, "Did you know it was your mother's birthday today?" "No," said Mary. It's in two months; why?" "Well, I just wanted to let you know," I said, "and she is dressed to kill, and I do mean it; she is, and you need to play along." "Okay," said Mary. "But it will be tough as shit to do it."

"Well, don't swallow your tongue when you see her. And yes, I know it will be tough, but you only have to fake it for a few more hours, got it?"

And at least I got a smile out of her. The kids were finished, and I helped her put them down, whispering, "Take a deep breath, blow it out, and get a 'special cup' of coffee before you look her way. You will need it."

I left the room, grabbed my 'special coffee,' with just a touch of whiskey to sell the drinking, and went to sit down, distracting Hellene from Mary coming out.

Mary walked out of the bedroom and quickly turned to the kitchen. She grabbed her 'special coffee' with just a touch as well, and then she turned and saw Hellene, dressed to kill, as I said. She said, "Happy birthday, Mom, and don't you look special today? Anyone that I know?" And she laughed as she sat down.

Hellene goes, "Sadly, no, but I just felt like celebrating a little bit anyway. It's not too much, is it?"

"Not in the slightest; sometimes you just have to wear what makes you feel like a queen." I thought, *A little thick, but I think it worked on her ego. And she now thinks she is the 'Queen of Darkness,' which could work to my benefit, especially if she gets careless. Not bad, Mary, not bad at all!*

I said to Mary, "Well, the babies have been fed, so we have a little less than four hours until feeding time again. Get Red moving, and I will go start loading the truck. Then, looking at the thermometer by the back door, I grabbed my heavier coat.

I'll see you two in a few. Oh, and tell Red I laid out steaks for tonight. Steak and baked potatoes sound great for dinner. And when dinner is done, the dogs will feast on tidbits and bones." I pulled my coat on and grabbed my two additional 9mm and five more clips, hidden by the door, just in case, which easily fit in my jacket. And out the door, I went.

As they walked out the door, I had the truck full. Hellene was at the door, waving goodbye as we pulled away. The minute we were out of sight, I pulled over and jumped out of the truck, handing one of the 9mms from under the seat.

"Mary, there is one more under there, and I know you won't be afraid to use it. Drive to Margie's and fill Red in on everything as you go. Now move. I have work to do. You know the rule: not until I call," I said. And I was in the brush and gone like I had never even been there.

Red looked at Mary and said, "Hellene is not Hellene, right?" All Mary said was, "Yes, and Joe is going to Kill her before she kills the kids. That is all I know, but if there is a man in this world that I trust, it is Joe.

And I know you do, too. So, hang on. We are doing the most challenging part: waiting!" Then, *something Joe said, Wait, Joe, last night. . ."* Joe said, "The 'Devil' will have one less minion when he is done. And that she will die, slowly and painfully." And then, more to herself, she said, "The dogs!!! That's why he made a point of me telling you he left steaks out for dinner, because he figures, and he is probably right, she will bait them into another room, long enough to get the kids out of the house and into the barn.

Where, (She crosses herself) he figures she will ritualistically kill each of them, and whatever else she has planned, I don't even want to think about it. Here is Margie's, and we have to be calm and tell her we are going to deliver the spinners once Joe walks over or calls. Other than that, it is up to us to be 'cool' under pressure. And as Joe and God say, 'Got it?'"

Red crosses herself and says, "God help Joe, and yes, I got it."

I was at the house in minutes, which was good because Hellene was already in motion. She had the dogs trapped in Red's room, and they were going crazy. But she knew if she shot them, it would echo up the valley like thunder and be sure to alert someone that something wasn't quite right.

She grabbed both sleeping children, still wrapped in their blankets, and headed to the barn, as I hoped she would because a lot of my plan depended on it. She walked in, shut the door, and locked it but didn't check the others, all of which I unlocked this morning. She looked at the piece of plywood the girls had used for the star mounting of the coconuts and said, "How nice of them to do my job for me."

She pulled out black chalk from her bag and outlined the pentagram with it. Then she checked her watch and said, "Right on time. Couldn't have done it any better, but being the 'Queen of Darkness' does have its advantages after all." *Way to go, Mary; it worked hook, line, and sinker; it really worked on her ego like I hoped it would*, I thought as I crept silently through the northeast door directly behind her.

As I moved slowly forward, one of the horses whinnied, and thank God she didn't turn, but she said, "Shut up, you old nag, or you are going to get the same as the dogs when I am through here. In fact, you're next, just for the Hell of it, and she laughed so evilly it made my blood run cold."

My samurai sword was right behind the stable fence pole, where I put it. I slowly placed it on the bales of alfalfa, where, at a moment's notice, it could take her head off at the shoulders, but that was not the plan.

She placed each baby on the pentagram, pulled her black volcanic glass knife out of her bag, and nicked each child's throat just deep enough for a drop of blood to seep out of the tiny wound. She touched the tip of her knife to both wounds and then licked off the blood.

And said to herself, "I am so glad I get all this blood to myself. I will be the 'Queen of Darkness' after this coup. Then she started her incantations to the Devil himself, the 'Prince of Darkness'!"

When she cut each of the babies, I almost took her head but thought of my promise to Mary. Slowly and painfully! And slowly and painfully, it would be. Focusing on that kept me sane, as the thought of that promise brought me back, and again, I was the man who was going to execute her. The protector of those two innocent children lying on that workbench. And even more importantly to me. My children, and as God is my witness, they are mine and Mary's to love until! And the ladies will never know about how she was using that piece of plywood, I swore to God!

As I listened, I knew from my studies and experience, an experience that I never thought I would ever have to think about again, that she was just about done with her ritual. She raised her glass knife to strike Christian first and then Hope second.

I swung my rope, and the loop caught her arms, head, and neck, and the knife dropped and stuck in the plywood, in the middle of the pentagram and between the babies, barely missing them.

Thanking God for his 'Guidance' of her glass knife.

I pulled her up until she was dangling with just her toes on the ground so as not to leave any marks on her neck. I tied off the rope very securely and picked up my sword.

Hellene's eyes followed my every step as I walked over to the pentagram, pulled down my pants, and peed on it. Washing part of it away so it lost the power she imbibed into it. Then I moved each baby off from the pentagram to the workbench, threw it on the floor, and peed on it some more.

Then I turned to her and quickly tied her hands together at her wrists, and then, using my second rope, I tied it to her bound wrists, threw the second rope over the rafter, and after pulling it tight and tied it off, I removed the first.

She laughed at me and said, "You bastard, you can't get away with this; he will know as soon as I am dead." Then she laughed again and spit in my face. And to piss her off, I didn't even give her the satisfaction of wiping off as I slowly ran the tip of my sword across her throat without cutting the skin. So that she knew she was mine to kill.

And she screams, "Go ahead, you fucking coward, kill me. He will know, and he will know where to come to find you."

I looked at her with an all-knowing smile. "Do you really think I don't know that? If you think that, you are more of a fool than I actually thought you were," I said.

Then, without further adieu, using my sword, I very carefully cut open her blouse to see just what she kept hidden under there. And there it was, an amulet of some kind. Powerful, to be sure, since I could feel it through my sword. Using the sword, I lifted the amulet over her head and laid it in my piss, where she could hear it sizzle until it dried out.

Then I said these words to her, "Bitch, you come into my home to not only kill but to ritualistically kill 'My' children, given to me, to protect by God himself. Now you shall die as I promised Mary, and by now, Red knows as well. Do you want to know how you are going to die so no one will ever know you ever existed? You see, you fucked with the wrong man, 'Queen of Darkness'! I probably know more about the dark side than you even knew existed. You are but a child hanging in front of a true master of the 'Dark Side of Man.'"

The fear, though she tried not to show it, was evident on her face. "Oh, and you never answered my question, did you? No, I don't think so. You want to know what is going to kill you."

Even if you don't really care, I am going to tell you anyway. "I speak ten languages, I have a photographic memory, and I have three Ph. Ds. One is in psychology, and my thesis was titled "The Dark Side of Man." Another is in physiology. This basically means I know every single pain point on your body and how to stimulate your brain in a way that you feel that pain and I mean excruciating pain without any physical damage to the body.

The last Ph.D., which I am only one of three men who earned the degree, painfully, I must say, is in the 'Ancient Art of Witchcraft and Associated Torture,' which is illegal in almost all countries. And I can even talk to God, wolves, and other animals. In fact, here in the dead of winter, I can call up at least a dozen or so rattlers to slowly kill you with their venom. But no, that would be too fast and not near painful enough."

Now, there was no hiding it. She was so scared that pee ran down her legs. "Well, okay, since the 'Queen of Darkness' can't guess, I guess I am just going to have to tell you.

But first, I think a shot, no, maybe two are in order. I am going to enjoy this, but you, I am not sorry to say, you are not." So before I had my shots, I offered her one and brought it to her lips, and then as her lips reached for it, I said, "Sorry, too slow," and I shot it down. Then I took a heavy weight I just happened to have there and tied it to her feet. Then I pulled her up about a foot and a half or so so she could feel the weight pulling on her joints.

Then I walked over to the table and checked on the babies, and they were asleep. Then I said, "Good thing they are asleep because when you start screaming, they are going to scream as well. But maybe not, because you don't know it, but they are both Saviors sent by God himself. So, they might understand the need for your death, even as young as they are. The second shot went down so smoothly, it almost brought me to tears."

Then I asked her something so horrifying to her that she was shaking uncontrollably. I asked her, "If she knew what Holy water was. And the wail of 'Nooooo,' that she screamed, probably could be heard for miles if the wind hadn't been blowing down the canyon and up instead."

But just as she screamed, the wind died down, almost magically. And Mary said to Red, "Did you hear that? I think Joe's plan is working. That was a scream of total fear, not of pleasure."

Red goes, "I think you are totally correct. My skin shivered violently at the sound of it."

But I said, "But wait. Just for a second or so, the wind almost stopped. It was like God wanted Mary to hear you suffer. Well, maybe not, but too bad. It is down canyon now, and there isn't anyone for seven miles to hear it."

"Well," I said, "if you could look over your shoulder, you would see a horse trough with a cross in the bottom. A cross that has been recently blessed, and do you know what that cross does to all that water? Of course, you do. It makes it a trough that should fit your body and be full of Holy water. Won't that be nice and warm for a soulless thing like you?"

"Well, the ladies are waiting, and as you know, you should never keep a lady waiting. But you, Hellene, are an exception to that rule because you are anything but a lady. In fact, I am not even really sure what you are. But what I do know is that you are waiting for, I forget, oh yes, now I remember, to be executed, slowly and painfully. So shall we begin?" I asked, not waiting for an answer.

So, without any further verbal torture, I raised her up and slowly moved the pulley holding the rope and her. Then, as I promised, I slowly lowered her feet into the water. And as it boiled around them, she screamed, but there wasn't anyone there to hear her. Then I pulled her up and then lowered her into the water to her knees. Her screams were deafening, and just for the 'Heaven' of it, I screamed a guttural scream that silenced even Helene, but only for a second.

She screamed and cried like a baby as she looked down at what was left of her body in horror as I lowered her again, this time lowering her all the way to those magnificent breasts. And still the screams, the screams continued, because Holy water tends to keep the individual alive throughout the complete process. Finally, with only a third of her upper torso still left and alive, I thought of a question that just came Into my mind. Why, I don't know, but looking up and then at the 'Queen of Darkness,' I asked it. "Hellene, was it. . . worth it?"

Hellene, with terror-filled eyes and a raspy voice, asked, "What the Hell?"

Then I moved to a position where I was looking directly into those eyes and asked again, "Was it worth losing?"

Hellene, at the end of her sanity, screamed, "What the fuck are you talking about, you bastard?"

I shook my head, looked directly into her eyes, and said two words, "Your Soul."

Hellene's eyes widened as the reality of my question sunk in, and as her being went back to the night, the night she was given a choice by the Devil himself. A choice of forever living with all she ever wanted or life in prison for a crime of passion, of which the love of her life falsely convicted her.

I watched as all hope left her body, and her head fell forward in defeat. She said, "No! And He lied about everything as he took my soul. It's too late for me, but I wish, from the bottom of my heart, that I had said. . . No!

Years in prison are nothing compared to being the Devil's minion: Forever. The hate I generated, the death of innocents by my hand,

and finally, the corruption of young lives who, like me, chose, oh so wrongly."

Then, as her body stiffens with her head up, looking at the heavens, and knowing that her soul is gone, she quietly says, "God, please forgive me. Amen."

And then, with the ultimate statement, she screamed down at Hell and said, "Fuck you, Devil, Hell deserves you, and you, you Bastard, deserve Hell!"

Then, to me, she calmly and quietly pleaded, "Please let go of the rope; Where I am going, I am pretty sure; But God, anything but Hell again, even if I die like I never was."

Looking to the heavens and a final look at Hellene, I let go of the rope as her living remains dropped into the holy water, and the screams stopped, and the only thing that remained was her clothes and the rope and weight."

"Where am I?" I ask as I open my eyes and see stars and... "You are nowhere and everywhere." "Why?" "God sent you here, with the rest of us, because we are needed; you, Hellene, are needed as I, Death Walker, am, and we wait until called by Joseph. Joseph killed me and saved me, as he did you, Hellene."

I picked up my last shot, tilted it back, and swallowed hard. Then I gently picked up the babies and quickly took them into the house and put them to bed, and I was right. They slept right through it. I let the dogs out, and they took their places by the beds, looking sheepish.

And I said, "Anyone can make a mistake; just don't let it happen again." For some reason, I was sure they understood me. Then I thought, they are part wolf. *Coal*, I thought, *you can hear me, can't you? Coal* thinks *yes, and so can Snow. At first, we thought it was strange, but after the wolf attack, you became clearer.*

Then Snow thought to me. *Your mate was very pleased with you last night. What?* I thought. Snow thought, *You know what I just thought, she was delighted. You did well!* I blushed. *You listened? Only for a while, and* she smiled and thought, *I hope someday to be as pleased.* Coal thought, *Once the pups, who understand you now but will understand sooner than later; then Snow, we can look for mates to 'please and be pleased' at that time. I also look forward to the day, but our duty is here until the youngsters can take over. But even then, we will always be there when needed.* I, still blushing, said, "Try and sleep next time, okay?"

Then I plugged in the phone and called Margie, and she answered. I said, "Is Mary there? If so, please put her on. I heard her rush to the phone, and I said these words, "It is finished, 'Slowly and Painfully,' come home." Mary dropped the phone and ran out of the house with Rose closely on her heels. They jumped into the truck and, within a few short minutes, slammed on the brakes in the yard.

As Red and Mary ran in the front door, Mary made a beeline for the cradles, and Red just stopped with uncertainty in her eyes. Then we both heard Mary yell to the heavens, "Thank you, God!" Then she turned to me and asked, "You are all right, right?"

"Yes," I said, and I will, I think, tell you about it all in the future. It is something that does not really need to be known if you understand it. Mary said, "But yes, someday, I want all the details of that 'Bitches' death, okay?"

I said, "As you wish, but just know, it will remain in your mind for the rest of your life, and I can say so from not just this experience, understand?"

Mary says, "Yes, my love. I will consider that when and if I ask."

And then I took control. "Ladies," I said, "I want everything and anything she brought with her, and anything of hers including the bedding, mattress, suitcases, anything she might have actually even touched that we can't really clean, has to be destroyed by fire."

Then, Mary and Red started gathering anything and everything related to Hellene and were throwing it in a pile outside the back door, but something about Hellene nagged at my subconscious. Then I knew what it was, and I yelled, "Stop!" to Mary and Red and said, "Come here quickly."

They were there in a second, and Mary, with eyes wide, yelled, "What is wrong?" "Nothing, I hope," I said. Then I asked, "Have either one of you seen her purse?" Red and Mary both said, "No." Mary said, "I know she brought it in with her from the airport, but since then, I haven't seen it."

Then I say, "The only other time I have seen it was when she was trying to make that telephone call late that night, and she had a small book in her hand: probably her 'little black book,' if I had to guess. So, it is here somewhere. We have to find it now, and if you do find it, under any circumstances, don't touch it! I will handle it if it is found.

Now, we all search the house from top to bottom quickly but systematically and thoroughly. Start with the bedroom first. Look in every place twice, if needed, to ensure it isn't in some little 'hole in the wall,' so to speak. I will start here, although I think she would have kept it near and dear. Now start and pray that we find it. Because I need something I think is in it, and I need it badly to finish this all off."

I found nothing in the living room or kitchen, and I didn't really expect to find anything. I saw nothing in either closet or even in the little library/study room I had for books and to pay bills. And then I heard the sound I was hoping for.

"Found it," yelled Red. I ran toward the bedroom where Mary and she were searching. She was smiling like the Cheshire cat and pointing toward a loose floorboard. I ran into the kitchen to get my sword, which I seem to be using on a somewhat regular basis now. I used it to move the floorboard out of the way slowly. And right there it was her purse, even red and black. What a coincidence.

I used my sword to pick it up and take it into the kitchen. I looked around and then grabbed a cookie sheet and dumped her purse out very carefully so as not to really disturb anything I hoped I would find. The cookie sheet and anything else of minor or no value in the purse would be destroyed with some leftover acid, which I happened to have; imagine that, from an etching job.

Then, with my sword in hand, I slowly separated the wheat from the chaff, as they say, and found two significant pieces that I knew were valuable. Very valuable to me, or let's say valuable to the world, and leave it at that.

The first was Hellene's 'little black book,' and the second, and most important, a plain wooden box. From the weight of it, it was probably a lead-lined box that no one would question, especially if it held a piece of jewelry, like an 'amulet,' for example.

I looked at the ladies and said, "Jackpot!" And then I said, "I tried to figure out how she traveled on an airplane with an amulet that powerful, that it could transmit a signal anywhere in the world. A signal that would indeed affect the electronics of, say, an airplane would have to be shielded anywhere near an airport.

Then, thinking about the amulet, one long-lost thought popped into my mind. Silver! Silver doesn't kill the minions, but it slows them down significantly. If it works on minion power, why not on the amulet?

The amulet, damn it, where is it, and I thought, *the barn*. Running out the back door and into the barn, there it was: the amulet, just where I had left it in my dried piss on the defiled pentagram right next to her black volcanic glass knife.

I grabbed the knife, stuck it in my back pocket, and then used my sword to pick up the amulet. I then headed back to the house. I looked for and found the leather bag I use when I am in the woods, and now it would work just perfectly for what I intended to use it for. And now I need silver, and the only silver I have is my mom's 'silver.' I knew that it was the real thing: sterling silver. Now Joe, think about how to do this the best way. Buried in silver, that's it, as I stuffed some of the silver polishing cloths, a pie scoop with a wide blade, and several large spoons into my bag.

Then I stopped, thinking about *the box*. The box she used to travel with shielded the amulet's power from interfering with the airport's electronics and needs to be examined. Then, using my sword again, I picked up and dropped the amulet into Hellene's wooden, lead-lined box and closed it. Using my sword, I detected a significant shift in power, but it was still a strong power.

Then, I opened the box, removed the amulet, and covered it with some of Mom's silver; the emitted power that I felt with my sword significantly diminished. Then, looking at the ladies, I said, "My thoughts are that the lead-lined box blocks electronics, but silver blocks whatever other power the amulet emits, so to be on the safe side, the amulet, using the silver pie scoop, was placed in the box, then closed and placed into the bag."

Then I said to myself, "Sorry to use your silverware this way, Mom, but it is needed in the worst way." I dumped the rest of the silver from the box into the bag and closed it tightly with the drawstring. Using my sword to test, I put it against the bag and could barely sense any power, although some power was still evident, which worked perfectly in my plans: some, but not so much as to track easily.

Then, looking at her 'little black book' lying on the table, I said, "There it is, my fine wife and friend. That book is the secret to her final, total disappearance. That and a call our group actress, Mary, is going to make in just a few minutes as I get ready for about a two-day trip, which I will explain to you later."

Then, as the ladies worked in the house to find and remove anything, 'Hellene,' I went to the barn, where I gathered up the pentagram plywood, her bag, the rope, and what was left of Hellene's clothes, took everything outside, and added it to the pile the ladies were making.

Red grabbed the acid, poured it on the pile of garbage from Hellen's purse, and literally dissolved everything it touched. Meanwhile, Mary went back into the house, gathered up all the trash and debris from the house, and threw them in the pile as well.

The pile, steaming from the acid poured on it, immediately caught fire, and within minutes, nothing but a black pile of soot lay there, which was already blowing down the valley in a nice, strong wind.

With that accomplished, we headed into the house for a well-deserved shot, and Red said, "Mr. Joe, I know I have said it before, and as much as I hate to say it because I know I will repeat it in the future: 'You will never cease to amaze me.'" Then she raised her glass, looked at me, and said, "There is no more to say."

Red, Mary, and I raise our glasses and, in one grand swallow, empty them. Then I say, "Before Mary makes her call, I have something to show you. You will be shocked, but you have to know, and what I show you will have to be destroyed should I ever, well, you get the idea."

So, as they waited in the kitchen, I quietly, so as not to wake up the children, went into our bedroom and then into the closet to my 'hidden' safe, the combination, which I have to disclose to the ladies, is on the back page of the Bible on the mantel.

I opened the safe and pulled out a cedar box, of course, made by me. I took it out into the kitchen and opened it up for the first time to anyone but myself. Then I said, "I here is my mystery life, which only one other person knows of, and that is Frank." I reached in and pulled out a file folder.

"Inside are three PhD diplomas," and as they read the titles, they start to understand how I know what I know. Then, pulling out another folder, I said, "This one has at least a dozen passports for regular and some relatively obscure countries, all with different names, dozens of driver's licenses from at least thirty states and several countries, and at least a dozen commendations from numerous intelligence agencies, both domestic and international, two US presidents, and several from religious entities including the Vatican, with a signature from unbelievably high up."

Then, after a long pause, I say, "I also hold a security clearance higher than the president himself."

As they sit there in awe, I continue and say, "Mary, you have a job to do. It is really straightforward. I have looked in her little black book, and there is only one underlined contact, which says 'emergency,' and that is the number you will call.

The bag, filled with silver and the amulet, will be right beside the phone, so it should transmit at least a weak enough signal to the 'thing' on the other end of the line for some ID to be made.

You will say in a very low, breaking up, and quiet voice, 'Hellene here. I can only talk for a second as I am at the Durango airport, under the name, '...'! No, go here on 'you know who'; girl anyway; family removed, and bodies disposed of 'permanently'; heading for Albuquerque; short turnover, plane to plane for Delaware. Out.'"

"Showtime, Mary!" Then I say, "Baby, I know you can do it. Just put yourself in her mind just one more time. Then the babies will be safe as we can make them after all of this. Now, please do it. The number is, imagine, 666-999-6666."

Mary picks up the phone, takes a deep breath, then a second, and dials. The voice on the end says, "Your emergency?"

Then Mary says just what I had told her to and how to say it. Then the voice says. "Noted!" And then the line went dead, and Mary hung up the phone.

Mary, with relief on her face, quietly said, "I need a shot, maybe two!"

Then I hugged her and said, "You did very well, just like I knew you would. Now your part is done. Now I finish it. By the way, do you two like the color turquoise on a truck like ours?"

As Red was pouring the drinks, I carefully removed the amulet from the bag and placed it in its unique travel box, then into the silver-filled bag. Next came her little black book, followed closely by the rest of Mom's silver. I pulled the drawstrings on the bag closed and placed the bag, along with the gloves, in a small safe I had in the library, closing and locking it.

I was going to put Hellene's knife in the bag of silver with the amulet, but I stopped, only knowing for some unknown reason that it would be 'necessary' as I went back into the bedroom and put the cedar box and files, along with the knife back in my safe.

Then, I quickly explained to the girls over beers, for a welcome change and a bunch of elk sandwiches, that I was going to go down to Farmington, where my red truck was via a local paint-in-a-day shop, was to be painted.

I will then spend the night at a local dive I know down by the Animas River. Then, a good friend of mine, who owes me many a favor, will take me out in his boat to the deepest point in Navajo Dam, where Hellene's amulet and the other things of hers will rest in a fireproof/waterproof safe on the bottom for life, as it will sink deeply into the ever-deepening silt to be lost until the end of time.

Then, he would drop me off at the paint shop to pick up my truck and swear on a stack of Bibles that he hadn't seen me in decades, especially since the truck was in another person's name, and the same name was on my license. Then, he would go home.

"Oh," I said, "Red, do you have plenty of sunflower seeds? I want to try an experiment I just thought of."

CHAPTER FIFTEEN

The truck looked great, especially since I decided to have it two-toned, turquoise, with a gold metallic roof, hood, and tailgate. As I pulled into the driveway after my two-day trip south to Farmington, I wondered just what the ladies would think. Well, they melted and were amazed that I was creative and brilliant.

Then Red, always the most curious of the two, said, "Well, here are the sunflower seeds. Are you going to grow them out in the snow now to impress us more?" They burst into laughter.

I said, "No, but please go into the house and watch. You may see a strange event, which I am not even sure will work. Now go."

As they go inside, I go to the barn, grab a shallow pan and a chair, and walk over to Red's garden. Then, I place the pan on a corner post of the garden, fill it about a third of the way with seeds, put the chair in the sun, and basically wait.

In about ten minutes, two pinion jays landed, and then they took the seeds away and ate them. I sit there quietly, and after the third visit, they stay and eat. Then, to test my theory, I think, *So, do you like the seeds?*

The birds flutter up but land down again and look at me like I'm a ghost or something. Then it happened. The female thought, *Yes, but you are thinking to us, why?*

And the male, not to be left out, thinks, *You destroyed her, didn't you? My name is Jose, and this is Fran. And you are Joe.*

I thought, *Right on both counts. Yes, I destroyed her, and then I took what was left away. Do you mind?* Fran pipes in and thinks, *No, she was…* As she looks at Jose, he shakes his head, Yes. Fran continued and said, '*EVIL.*' *And Joe, we know all that live in this valley and are very happy to live here. And since you asked, the seeds are delicious. And both ladies . . . right?*

I thought, *yes. They are adorable, especially when it is cold and snowy.* Then, thinking again, *Fran and Jose, you say that you know everyone who lives in the valley, correct? Yes,* thought Jose, *especially those with seeds!*

Then I have one request and one question. Is that okay? Again, Fran looked at Jose for approval and thought, *Yes. We will answer if we can; that is the best we can do.* I thought, *That is all I would ever expect. First, since we are the first ones in the valley, could you let me know if a stranger enters the valley?*

It will have to be me since, because of God, I am the only one who can talk to you.

We understand. I continue. And if for some reason I am not here, make a wild ruckus in front of one of the windows. Do you know Ruckus?

Jose thinks *We are pinion jays, and 'ruckus' is our middle name. The other Jays nearby are Stellar Jays, who are very stuck up but still good birds.*

Thinking again, *Can you speak to other birds?* Jose thought… *Yes. That is, except those like hawks and eagles and such that try to eat us. As for the night, the owls have great eyes, and they know all that is happening over an even broader territory than us.* I thought, *I know it may sound strange, but are there birds out there that are "EVIL," like Fran mentioned about the 'thing' that I destroyed.*

Jose looked at Fran, and she shook her head. He looked at me and thought, *Yes, there are, and we are always on the watch for them. They are always looking for, I know it sounds strange, but for babies that are from God himself. And it seems like they have been in the area over the last few months or so. So, your answer is yes.* But he continues thinking *since you killed her, there have been fewer and fewer of them around, almost back to normal. But typical for them is where there is usually dead food. That is what they crave.*

He thought, *Why do you ask?* As I thought, I knew that Jose and Fran knew what I was thinking.

Jose thinks, and his thought was, *Now you are wondering if we are trustworthy, right?*

I thought, *Yes, are you? Just tell me so I know. We are,* thought Fran. *And we will keep your secret.*

I know this from your thoughts. Thank you. I only have a few friends; now I have two more.

Then Fran thought. *As we now know, you want us to keep watch. So that you know, we will be there for you and them. What are their names? Christian and Hope Everlasting,* I thought, and as I took a deep breath, and thought, *Thank you.* Jose thought *we were just birds, but we would do our best.*

I thought, *If you see anything out of the ordinary, especially a flock of "EVIL" birds, give me the alarm signal. If I am not around, break a window with a rock if need be. I will tell the ladies that this is the signal to head to the church as fast as possible.*

Fran thought solemnly, *God be with you, and we will watch and let others that are reliable know to watch and warn as well.*

I thought, *Thanks, and God bless! Then it is a deal. We will keep the seeds coming. By the way, do you like cracked corn as well? Fran's favorite!* Thought Jose.

My last thought was, *I have to go now. Enjoy your seeds; the cracked corn will be coming soon. And Fran, I hope you have many chicks. Fran cocked her head to the right and asked, How did you know?*

I just smiled and thought, *I have 'feelings' about things. Enjoy!*

Then I picked up my chair, retrieved the pan, and headed to the house. Once in the house, I said to Red, "Make sure you always have plenty of sunflower seeds, and I will buy some cracked corn as well. Fran loves cracked corn.

And now listen. If strangers enter the valley, I have asked Fran and Jose, the pinion jays, to give us a heads-up by causing a 'Ruckus' outside a window. But for some reason, and I am not here, if the pinion jays or any other bird grabs a stone and throws it at or through the front window, take the children immediately to the church. Do you understand?"

"Yes," said Mary and Red. "I will explain to you later, okay? Now, let's enjoy the rest of the day and evening."

I went to the cabinet, poured three shots, and said, "The experiment worked. Boy, did it work! Ladies, would you like to join Dr. Doolittle for a shot? But this may call for two. No, I know it will call for two, and you both can close your mouth now, except for your shot and maybe a question or two.

Oh, and the pups are just now starting to understand me, according to Coal, but they should pick it up quickly. At least, that is what he thought to me. So please join me! You look like wooden soldiers standing there."

They both looked at each other, came to the table, shot the poured shot, and indicated a second was in order. They hit that one just as fast, and then the questions began.

"Now, it is your turn, Mary, but so that you know, Snow was happy you were so pleased the other night and hopes she will be that 'pleased' with her mate someday."

Mary slowly says, "Okay, so Snow thinks I was 'well pleased. ' Would you care to expound on that comment?"

"Well, no, actually," I continued, as I told Snow, "Please, just go to sleep next time. And she responded by thinking, of course, that she would try. And then Coal thought to Snow, we both are looking forward to our time to come, but we have our duty, and until the pups are up to the guarding, it is up to us, but even then, it is our responsibility until our deaths. Understood? Yes, thought, Snow, I know and fully agree.

But it was still fun to hear her so happy with her mate, don't you think, Coal? Coal was quiet for a moment. Then he thought they had worked hard to reach this point. Moments like that are to be treasured for life, but Snow, we messed up with Hellene when we fell for her ruse like pups. We will never let that happen again. You are right, Coal, thought Snow. Never again. I will die and give my last breath for these four, well, five. Red is a very special-hearted female, and I trust her like the others.

"I agree," said Coal, "all five, it shall be."

And finishing my talk with the dogs, I said, "At that point, they both put their heads down and slept, what I call the 'Nam' sleep. And I guarantee it will never happen again."

I said, "Well, speak or forever hold your piece, Red. But first, I think another big one is in order. Besides, I think Mary is wondering how to keep quiet from now on."

Red and I laughed our heads off as I hit the nail on the head.

Mary said, "Funny, very funny! I am so glad I made your day," as she actually smiled and said, "I guess if that is all I have to worry about, especially since I am still a virgin, I can't imagine what they might actually hear when the real action starts."

I still don't think I have ever seen her so red in my life. Damn, I enjoyed that shot.

Then Red, through her tears at what the dogs thought, takes her shot slowly and says thoughtfully, "Damn, you can actually talk with animals, or at least think with them. And now you have them guarding over us; God is great! And their names are Fran and Jose? Will wonders never cease around this 'little bit of heaven.' So, what else?"

"Well," again, I said, "they will watch after the valley and let the birds that don't eat them know to watch as well. They are going to spread the word to the owls who fly at night and in a much larger radius. And they were pleased that I took out the EVIL from the valley and thanked me. They will also keep a close watch on EVIL birds, like I said earlier.

And well, except Hellene, or what little is left of her, is swimming with the fishes in Navajo Dam at about the four-hundred-foot depth level and should be well buried in the silt by now. And no one knows I was there. Richard Carver stayed at the hotel, down by the river, had his truck painted, and left town.

Mary said, "It looks like Saturday is a go for the baby shower and Joe's little guy thing with the pony keg. So tomorrow, we deliver the spinners, come wind or snow, or more likely both, but the babies come with us this time."

And tomorrow, I said, I think I will look at my Christmas presents again. I have a strange feeling, and you two know about my feelings, that there is something in those three objects that I should know more about. And I intend to find out just what it is." Then I say, "And Red. No matter that Hellene was the 'devil's bitch', if you ever want to make that dinner again, I will never complain. Oh, and Mary, just so you know, she fell for the 'Queen of Darkness,' hook, line, and holy water. Can I get a hallelujah!"

Hallelujah rang out as three shot glasses hit the table at the same time. Dinner was great, and the wine hit the spot with the chicken hot off the grill, along with the last three ears of corn smothered in Red's homemade butter. And her green beans with her special rolls, what a meal.

We all needed that after the last few days, especially with the ending that worked out to a tee. As I thought about it, *I felt good about how all of it was executed. That does not mean that something wasn't missed. It was nothing but that in an 'execution,' especially with the execution of one of the 'Prince's' top minions. The potential for even a tiny, missed detail was always a possibility.*

I am sure, and if there is an expert on this earth that knows this adversary, it is me. I know it is going to be an uphill battle, and I will have to fight it every step of the way, so help me God.

Then I say to the ladies, "Those 'presents' are saying to me two things. First, 'study and learn,' and secondly, 'all is not what it seems.' So with 'study and learn' and 'all is not what it seems' as predicators,' I will begin what I feel has the potential, no will actually change, many, if not all of our decisions going forward. Thursday morning, and you both know I think better first thing in the morning, I will take on that challenge. That leaves Friday as wind spinner delivery day! Won't the neighbors be surprised?

While all seemed well in the Everlasting house, the depths of hell weren't quite as relaxed. First, the massive meteor strike on Christmas Eve resulted in the deaths of so many lovely evil women, men, and children. Second, there is a lack of any new saviors that have been sent, and if sent, they are not being found and destroyed. Or better yet, at least brought back to hell itself, to well, be his to feast upon and get stronger after the meteor fiasco.

Finally, the loss of contact with Hellene, his number three in line to sit beside him on his throne of skulls, although much lower. She had always thought of herself as his number one choice for 'Queen of Darkness.' And her utter love for herself. Disgusting! And in her mind, he knew that she thought that she, Hellene, would take his throne one day.

What a fool! But she had something a lot of the others didn't have. She had a man's guts to stand up to him, not for very long, mind you, but she still did it, and it made her . . . enjoyable at times. But that damned area where she was on a mission was so laden with silver, making communication nearly impossible. He found it incredible that she did complete her mission and reported, although fragmented. And then just literally disappeared off the face of the earth.

But gone she was, and minions met their matches and died, more than he would like to admit. It was pretty often that he would have to go to the 'surface' to clean up a mess, which irked him beyond belief. But he still had an ace in the hole in the area. And that 'ace in a hole' was a man from the local Ute tribe.

But the problem with him is that he has always been a loner, and even being the Devil, I actually know very little about him except that he is now a Colorado state patrol officer, moving up the chain of command with the title of 'Chief' being his ultimate goal. Which, to me, makes him even more critical.

So, all in all, losing Hellene was a loss. But others could easily take her place: for example, that blond vixen, Shellene. Now, there was a sexy and intelligent woman he could count on without any, well, almost any, doubt. Ah, here she comes now. I'll bet ten souls to one; she already knows about Hellene and is vying for her position.

He laughed to himself and swallowed a full cup of fresh blood. As it dripped down his chin, she licked it off. "Your Majesty, you did that just for me, didn't you?" said Shellene. Why yes, yes, I did. And what brings you to see me, my 'dearest'?" asked the Prince."

"Are the rumors of Helene not making it back true? If so, I shall just so miss that 'bitch'!" laughed Shellene.

And the Prince said, "I figured you would," as they both laughed out loud, in a very evil yet sultry way, as she climbed into his lap.

Meanwhile, in the Everlasting house, it was Thursday morning. After a fine breakfast, including special coffee, eggs, and excellent hash browns, I found myself, Red, and Mary sitting in the living room with my three gifts of interest laid out in front of me.

I said, "With 'study and learn,' and 'all is not what it seems,' as predictors and as my determining factors on which gift to research first. I am going to pick the gift that I think is the 'least' likely to make or break a decision.

My choice with 'study and learn' as a guide would be the book. But with the other predicator of 'all is not what it seems' taken into consideration', I chose the red wool shirt.

I picked it up and held it up to the light. I first looked at the back and then the front. As I examined the front, I stopped. In the left front breast pocket was what appeared to be a hole, and it seemed to be a bullet hole.

Inside the pocket was a small pocket Bible with a bullet hole. In the Bible, there was a silver dollar dated 1900, which also had a hole. It was wrapped in a small paper sleeve nestled in the Book of Revelation. All of us had an involuntary shiver when I said, "Revelation."

Then I said to Red and Mary, "Well, we now know the approximate date of when the man possibly got the Bible. And whoever he was, that Bible in his pocket probably saved his life more than likely; who knows? The bullet probably knocked him off his feet or his horse hard enough that he appeared dead to his assailant." But then, as I looked closer, hidden right behind the Bible was a folded letter in a yellowed envelope with no stamp, just the number two on the front.

Red said, "Well, open it."

I said, "No because it's number two.' And if you are going to 'study and learn,' you should, hopefully, start at the beginning." Mary says, "That makes sense to me; let's move on to the second present that you feel you should open."

That left two gifts of the set of three left to go. Mary goes, "Okay, Joe, which one is next?"

"Okay," I said. Again, with 'study and learn' and 'all is not what it seems' as guidelines, the 30-30 seemed to fit the best with the two predictors. So, with that said, the rifle was next in line to examine." As I looked at it as it lay there, I wondered, and I said, "Why would someone maintain the working parts in very workable condition yet leave what could easily be a fixable stock?"

Red says, "Beats me. Please pick it up and check it out like you did with the shirt. Use your intuition, which has been guiding you all along.

Then, using Red's guidance, without further speculation, I picked up the gun and started an inch-by-inch inspection of it from the end of the barrel to the butt of the stock. The barrel was as he had seen before, in great shape for a weapon of this age, including the end sight. The serial number was 101, which indicated that this was not only an old gun but a rare one as well.

But upon further inspection, I said, "The split in the stock runs from the metal band connecting the barrel and action to the stock all the way to the butt plate on the end of the stock. There was nothing new there I hadn't seen upon my first cursory inspection on Christmas Day.

So, I pulled out my scout knife, which I had had since I was eight, and used the screwdriver blade to release the stock from the barrel and the action. Again, nothing out of the ordinary except some dust and gun oil build-up on both the metal and wooden parts. The action was fully functional, with, again, just some dust buildup from not being cleaned in what was probably quite a while.

Mary then said, "Well, that just leaves the stock itself. And the only thing holding the two parts of the stock together is the butt plate." And since it was the last place to look, and since I would have to remove the butt plate anyway to glue and refinish the stock, I removed the two screws holding the butt plate to the stock. As most gun owners know, there usually is a bored-out hole at the end of the stock, especially with older guns, and this rifle was no exception. But the exception was it contained another yellowed envelope, identical to the first, except it had the number 'three' on it.

"The plot thickens," I said. Now, with two yellowed envelopes and only one gift to review, the book on the history of the 30-30 was the last and only choice. I picked it up and started examining the last and final of the three gifts. It had several paper bookmarks highlighting specific features of the weapon, such as cleaning and sighting in at specific distances using the adjustable sights.

But the bookmark on page 3 disclosed what I had hoped it would. The last yellowed envelope, as such, had the number 'one' on it. But this time, besides the 'one,' there was a signature and what appeared to be the final clue, written on it in a woman's gracefully flowing handwriting. Alice Chisolm signed it. And the note read, 'Only time will tell'.

I laid the letter with the number "one" on it beside the others in order, and Mary and Red were flabbergasted as Mary said, "Don't do anything at the moment. These letters have been basically hidden for decades, and a few more hours, or even days, will not make a difference at this point.

Tell you what, let's have a shot; just one, mind you. And then, since I just fed the kids, why don't we take them for a short walk? The day is excellent, with no wind or weather, and the fresh air will do us all good, including the dogs and the pups. What say you?"

As I sat there staring at the three letters, I said, "Good point. One shot it is, and the walk isn't a bad idea either. That way, I can let my mind detach from reality for a while and work on issues in the background, and for some reason, an answer seems to come to me."

"It is because," said Red, "you are a genius!" And she rolled her eyes, as only she can, and headed for the cabinet and poured. Then she said as she raised her glass, "To Alice Chisolm, and what she has to say in relation to 'only time will tell.'"

And after the shot went down, I said, "I am opening number three first when we get back." Then Mary looked at both of us and asked, "Why?"

I looked at her and thought for a moment or so and said, "Because 'only time will tell.' It takes time to get to three. That is it, plain and simple."

Mary just looked at me and said, "I will not ever underestimate your logic. So, let's get the kids ready. And I don't know about you two, but I am really looking forward to this walk. My mind needs a little bit of the solitude of nature to unwind the clock spring in my mind and body."

Red says, "I second that notion, and by the time we get back, everyone should be 'unwound.'"

The walk was just what everyone needed. As we headed north, Fran and Jose joined us. I thought, *Good morning to both of you and Fran. Did you enjoy the cracked corn?* Fran thought, *Oh my goodness, yes. Where did you get it?*

I thought, *And I remembered that I had bought some for Duke and Daisy's Christmas Day meal. They love it, probably even more than you do, Fran.*

Jose thought *she could smell cracked corn ten miles away. Fran thinks Jose is correct, although ten miles might be my limit. Are these the babies?*

I have Christian, and Mary has Hope. Blue for the boy and pink for the girl. The baby backpacks are from Red, and they were given to Mary and me as Christmas presents. So, what are you two out doing today?

Jose thought *It was just too lovely a day to hang around the nest. Then we saw all of you out for a walk and thought we would join you. We hope you don't mind.*

Not in the slightest. I told Mary and Red the signals just in case I was not around and there was a problem that they needed to know about. But, at the moment, it seems the danger has been reduced. So, I think we can relax and not worry as much.

Fran thinks, *Jose, it is time for more of that cracked corn. The closer it gets to egg time, the hungrier I seem.* Jose thought, *Yes, mother. As for the danger, I, too, feel, at least for the time being, that it has passed.*

And off they went.

Mary goes, "I take it your conversation was pleasant?"

"Why yes, but how did you know?" I asked. Well, you tend to concentrate in just a different manner since you have to 'think' about your conversation instead of speaking it," Mary said.

I said, "That is called a 'tell' in poker, and I will have to work on that not happening if I don't want anyone to know that I am having a mental conversation. Thanks for telling me. That could be dangerous in the wrong company. And now here is the end of the property and the turnaround point, and we still have to load the truck, again, at least for some of us, me in particular, before we go in and 'warm up.' Then the 'great' letter adventure begins anew."

Well, as we got to the barn, I said, "How about we just take Fr. John's spinner today, and then we can finish up the loading and delivering tomorrow. And I would bet that we might get just a tad bit of the 'good' stuff as a reward. Besides, the kids are still awake, and by the time we get back, they will be hungry and go down for a long while. And a long while of relaxation is something we all deserve. This walk was a good start, but a good deed like this sort of tops off the day. What do you ladies think?"

"I think it is a great idea." said Mary, and then Red said, "I totally agree. Let's get loaded and surprise the Father." The table was in the truck bed and tied down within minutes, the kids in the car seats, and we were off.

As we drove up into Fr. John's driveway, he came out and ran to the truck, beaming with excitement. He was like a mother hen and her chicks as we moved the wind spinner into his living room. He walked all around it like it was Christmas Day all over again. And with tears in his eyes, he thanked every one of us with a hug. And then he said to me. "Joseph, you are indeed a master. I will cherish this for as long as I live and then some.

So how about I break open a new bottle, saved just for special occasions like this, and we shall drink a toast to Joseph and Joseph. Craftsmen of the ages!"

Within minutes, we had our toast and were on our way home. That was a good thing because the kids were finally getting fussy, which usually meant two things: messy and hungry! And from the slight odor from the back seat, I am sure of at least one of the reasons.

We pulled in, and Red and Mary took the kids into the house. I fed the animals, did a quick cleanup of the stables, and went inside. The babies were cleaned up, dressed in their night clothes, and had just finished eating. Mary had them down, and they were asleep before she left the room. It had been a long day for them.

Then I said, "I was right about the 'good stuff,' wasn't I? But I didn't expect the 'excellent stuff,' and excuse my French, damn, that was 'excellent stuff.' And from the way you two savored every drop, I would say you totally agree with me." Then Red said, "I won't excuse my French. That was, damn, 'excellent stuff,' huh, Mary?" "Joe, do we have another spinner to deliver to the father?" asked Mary, smiling sweetly.

"But first, the letter," said Red.

I said, "I need one more of our just 'good stuff' first, then I open number 'three.'"

Red says, "Your wish is my command, and your willpower is so much greater than mine."

"Red, seriously, it isn't. It is just that I think this is going to be a much bigger deal than we might think. So, pour woman, you are getting slow in your old age," I said with a big smile. The shots were poured, and of course, after a comment like that, I am glad that I even got one. And I said a toast, "To Alice Chisolm, and what she wrote, 'only time will tell.'" Three shot glasses were raised and clinked together, and three were right back on the table.

We adjourned to the living room, and after we were all seated, I picked up envelope number 'three.' I carefully opened it and unfolded the parchment paper slowly because it was so old and very brittle. I took a deep breath as I read the first words of the letter out loud to Mary and Red. Words that I will remember forever:

"Dear Joseph Everlasting,

I hope this letter finds you in good health and . . ."

The end...

ABOUT THE AUTHOR

A. Ben Bacon was born in Stevens Point, Wisconsin, in July 1953. When he was five, his family moved to Farmington, New Mexico, where he lived for almost fourteen years. He was married to his first wife, Connie, there. Now, as a widower from his second wife, Doreen, of nearly eighteen years, he lives in Colorado with his partner of five years, Sandra Hays.

He has lived in twenty-six states and six countries during his lifetime. In January 1973, he enlisted in the US Navy, where he sailed on the USS Camden off the coast of Vietnam during the Vietnam War. After he left the US Navy, he went to the University of Utah, where he received his Bachelor of Science in meteorology in March 1979. In 1983, he joined the US Air Force as an officer. Subsequently, he became a typhoon chaser (hurricane hunter in the United States) flying as an aerial reconnaissance weather officer/instructor out of Guam, a US territory. To him, it was the job of a lifetime. To be a meteorologist and able to fly a four-engine turboprop C-130 Hercules into the eye of the world's worst storms was heaven on earth to him. During almost three years of flying into typhoons, he penetrated the eye of the typhoon 39 times, which awarded him three Air Medals. The Black Swan Squadron was inactivated on September 30, 1987. Upon squadron inactivation, Ben was accepted to the US Navy's prestigious Naval Postgraduate School, a NATO school located in Monterey, California, where he received his Master of Science degree in meteorology in June 1989.

Ben's love for the outdoors is a cornerstone of his life, a passion that led him to settle in the picturesque state of Colorado. His favorite pastimes include hiking, snow skiing, road trips, and fishing, all of which allow him to connect with nature and rejuvenate his spirit. When he's indoors, he indulges in a variety of creative pursuits, such as reading, writing, cooking, watercolor painting, and collecting barometers. These diverse interests reflect his multifaceted personality and his constant quest for new experiences.

While living in Colorado, in the summer and fall, he especially enjoys driving and four-wheeling his 1968 Jeep CJ5. He originally bought the Jeep several years ago for $400. After a lot of blood, sweat, and tears, it is now tearing up and down the jeep trails across Colorado. In the winter, Purgatory Resort, north of Durango, Colorado, is where he shreds powder and craves the moguls with family and friends.

Ben's family is the anchor of his life, and he cherishes every moment spent with them. He is a proud father to two sons, Anthony and Josh, and two stepsons, Scott and Jeff. His seven grandchildren, Ellie, Micah, Trinity, Damiel, Judah, Avery, and #7 Madison, bring him immense joy and laughter. And, of course, his daughters-in-law, Katie, Mel, and Amanda, are cherished members of his family. Their love and support were a constant source of strength for him throughout his life.

The Coming is Ben's first book in the series, initially published in 2019. The Coming Hunted, which will be published in late summer 2024. His first was Cam's Dragon, published in 2018.